MITCH DITKOFF

STORY TELLING FOR THE REVOLUTION

MAKING WAY FOR THE ULTIMATE UPRISING OF INSIGHT, WISDOM, AND LOVE

ADVANCED PRAISE

"Mitch Ditkoff knows that the real revolution comes from within and then extends outward to action. He writes with rare wisdom, depth, humor, and insight. Each story he shares has the capacity to inspire the rest of us to action that matters."
– Gail Larsen, Author of *Transformational Speaking: If You Want to Change the World, Tell a Better Story*

"This is a powerful and important book. When we have the courage to tell our stories, we form a bond with each other that no one can defeat or overwhelm. Mitch Ditkoff makes an indisputable case for the essential role of storytelling to create change."
– Susan Page, Director, San Miguel Writers Conference and Literary Festival

"What I love about *Storytelling for the Revolution* is the compelling way it liberates humanity's biggest untapped resource – our collective wisdom lurking just beneath the surface of our lives."
– Marshall Goldsmith, Author of *Triggers*, a New York Times best-seller

"Mitch taps into the deep well of our collective wisdom and reclaims the collective narrative for the greater good. *Storytelling for the Revolution* is a rallying cry for people to recognize their deep meaningful connections with others and reminds us that we are not alone. It is a groundbreaking work in its simplicity and profundity. An important, seminal work for our age."
– Michael Frick, CEO, Speaking.com

"Mitch Ditkoff's stories are beautiful and a huge encouragement for the rest of us to share our own stories with each other. This is what's needed these days –the authentic sharing of what we know to be true, based on our own life experiences and inner wisdom. Not fake news. Real news – the news of the heart."

– Cassandra Wilson, Grammy award-winning jazz and blues singer

"Today, I read the first six of the 40 stories in Mitch Ditkoff's *Storytelling for the Revolution*. Immediately, I felt my heart replace my mind and called out to my new wife that we had something delightful to read together in bed tonight. Big thanks to Mitch for helping me shift gears in the 80th year of my life. Anyone who can quiet themselves enough to pay attention to their own inner wisdom will find great value in this groundbreaking book."

– Tim Gallwey, Author of *The Inner Game of Tennis*
   and *The Inner Game of Work*

"Through Mitch Ditkoff's master storytelling we are welcomed under a big tent called humanity with stories that whisper truths, uniting and celebrating us all. His stories rumble deep from within, where cleverness meets humility and tragedy dances with angels. Mitch's stories inspire reflection while the field guide provides the step-by-step guidance needed for readers to mobilize the storyteller within and lead their own personal revolution."

– Doug Stuke , Director, Sales Excellence,
   The Hartford Insurance Group

"Mitch's stories have the power take us deeper into our own selves, encouraging us to pay closer attention to every aspect of our lives. *Storytelling for the Revolution* is an inspirational work to say the least. It is a book that has no timeline and will be here forever, changing lives, page by page."

– Sharon Jeffers, Author of *Love and Destiny, Discover the Secret Language of Relationships*

"Storytelling, like music, is a universal language that evokes shared emotions and connects us to each other. In Mitch Ditkoff's second book of stories, *Storytelling for the Revolution,* he deftly weaves tales that give vivid insight into our hearts and emotions, helping us interpret and understand our own lives in a very personal way. This book of stories, meditations of the human soul, will positively transform your life."

– Geri Presti, CEO and President, The Cleveland Music Settlement

"Stories are all about gathering personal and collective experience and knowledge. They gain meaning when the storyteller communicates with verve and creativity. In *Storytelling for the Revolution,* Mitch Ditkoff beautifully fulfills this promise and offers precise prompts for accessing the wisdom tucked inside the tale".

– David Gonzalez, award-winning storyteller, poet, and arts advocate

"I loved this book and will be sharing it with sacred activists around the world. I especially loved the way the author made the connection between revolution and revelation. Highly enjoyable."

– Kurt Krueger, President, Success Systems International

"A journey of a thousand miles begins with a single step."

— Lao Tzu

To Prem Rawat who has shown me what exists beyond story.

ACKNOWLEDGMENTS

• Prem Rawat • Evelyne Pouget • Emilia Ditkoff • Jesse Ditkoff • Barney Ditkoff • Sylvia Ditkoff • Phyllis Rosen • Catharine Clarke • Jo Ann Deck • Cathy Lewis • Kurt Kruger • Gail Larsen • Mary Jane Fahey • Marcus Villeca • Barbara Schacker • Christine Summers • Ron Brent • Val Vadeboncoeur • Scott Cronin • Robert Esformes • Sharon Jeffers • Craig Lennon • Elizabeth Lennon • Peter Blum • Carlos the Tour Guide • Zentenos • Café Rama • Mesa Grande • Mercado Sano • San Miguel de Allende • Woodstock, NY • All storytellers – past, present, and future

GO FUND ME DONORS

• Steve Kowarsky • Joe Belinsky • Charles Cameron • Gary Ockenden • Michael Frick • Lucinda Brown • Allen Feld • Paul Solis Cohen • Tim Williams • Joan Apter • Roddy Nierenberg • Joan Weinstein • Suzanne Elusorr • Marc St. Andre • Ita McAteer • Rita Rubin-Long • Eva Roha • Gilman Hanson • Ben Franschman • Barbara Locke • Brad Uffner • Rahul Sagar • Tom Carroll • Marsha Willis • Eve Baer • Elise Pittleman • Peter Buettner • Carola Polakov • Niels Lenz • Susan Page • Steve Gorn• Harvey Kaiser • Hakan Borgstroem • Reinhard Zueschang • Lise Turbide • Laurence Swift • Ron Brent • Margaret Hermann • Francoise Florsheim • J Leisch • Sam Magarelli • Chris and Daya McVittie • Lucy Scala • Sara Travers Gillett • Teresa Payne • Carl Hebeler • Claudia Watts • Chuck Frey • Thomas Workman • Prema Kaye • Henry Wyman • Craig Klawuhn • Jean Paul Peretz • Yvette Korrell • Debbie Leppla • Pamela Miles • Tina Lipson • Eve Ilsen • Dan Munter • Phil Noble • Adrienne Reid • Karen Cohn • Patricia Barrett • Roger Ellman • Yvonne Carrington • Bruce Segal • Ahman Khadra • Kathy Piehnert • Mary Haley • M Lolkema • Tim Hain • Carol Jaffe

COVER DESIGN

Marcus Villeca: www.rocketpigmedia.com

TABLE OF CONTENTS

PART ONE: THE STORIES

PART TWO: THE FIELD GUIDE

INTRODUCTION:
LET US GATHER AROUND THE FIRE

"Those who tell the story, rule the world."

–Hopi Indian saying

If you are wondering why I chose to call my book: *Storytelling for the Revolution* – a title some people might consider incendiary, inflated, or overly dramatic, here's the reason: *We need a revolution. We do.* But the revolution I'm inviting you to join is not a political one. It has nothing to do with a change of government, laws, sanctions, or social structures. It has everything to do with a change of *mind* and a change of *heart* and a change in the way we *communicate* with each other.

It doesn't take a genius to recognize that the collective narrative occupying the airways these days is a dark one – not all that surprising when you consider the sorry state of the

1

world and the "if it bleeds, it leads" mindset of the media: Bad news sells. It's true. But bad news is not the only thing worth reporting. Indeed, there is another kind of story that also needs to be heard – one that rarely makes it to the evening news. And that story is revolutionary – or could be – the story of how each and every one of us is a broadcast station of insight, wisdom, and love – three phenomena that have the power to transform what is happening on planet Earth.

I am not suggesting you airbrush out the bad news to contemplate your navel. I'm not asking you to become apolitical. All I'm asking you to do is pay more attention to another kind of news – one that can never be dominated by troll farms or spin-doctors. And do you know the most reliable source of that story? *You. Yes, you!* Inside of you, there is another kind of story occurring, another narrative, one that exists far beyond *late breaking* and *this just in*, one too rarely told. *I'm talking about the story of your life* – or, more specifically, the absolute Ground Zero of what you have learned and what you are learning, what you have felt and what you feeling, what you have seen and what you are seeing – even while the world burns down: Essence. Lessons learned. Insights. Moments of truth. Breakthroughs. Obstacles overcome. Personal tales of inspiration, kindness, resilience, love, meaning, vulnerability navigated, and the undeniable wisdom you have gleaned from your own life experiences. In other words, what makes you truly human, a *homo sapien* – meaning, "the one who knows."

Sages, masters, and elders may be the most historically recognized "keepers of wisdom," but they are not the only ones. The rest of us are, too. The thing is, we don't always know it. Our wisdom is often invisible to us. It is hiding. Unseen. Unacknowledged. And unexpressed.

And where our wisdom is hiding, more often than not, is in our *stories* – much like water hiding in underground springs. *Everyone* has wisdom inside of them. *Everyone*. Everyone has learned something profound, soulful, and timeless in this life. Everyone has something meaningful to share. And, when they share it, *in the form of story*, they have the potential to spark wisdom in others. Like, for example, in the following story, a brief retelling of an old Zen tale.

Once upon a time in feudal Japan, there was an old monk living in a monastery deep in the mountains. Ever since he was a small boy he had lived in this monastery and was considered by his fellow monks to be a most extraordinary soul. Every morning he would awake at 4 AM and meditate for two hours. Then he practiced calligraphy and prepared breakfast for the other monks. Every afternoon, he read the sutras and, when he wasn't chanting mantras or writing haiku, he worked in the garden. Silently, of course.

Years passed. Seasons came and went. And so did his youth. But no matter how much effort he made, the enlightenment experience that he so diligently sought never came. And so one day, in his 70th year, he decided to leave the monastery and return to the world. "Why should I continue with all these spiritual practices," he asked himself, "if they are not helping me reach my ultimate goal?"

Needing to earn a living, he soon got a job as a sweeper in a local cemetery. Every day he went to work. And every day he swept.

And then, one sunny day, three years into his new, non-monastic life, a stone he had just swept off the path smashed into a tree and split in two. And when it did, something in *him* split in two, cracked wide open – the kind of open that never closes again. Everything, suddenly, became totally clear to him. The enlightenment he had been seeking for 50 years had finally happened. *Just like that.*

The 40 stories you are about to read are 40 stones splitting in two – 40 examples of spontaneously occurring *moments of truth* – awakenings, both large and small, none of which have ever made it to the evening news. Some of them are from my own life. Some are from the lives of others. They are, metaphorically speaking, a kind of DaVinci code that offers clues to the encrypted wisdom lurking just beneath the surface of our life – the hard-to-communicate essence that ultimately defines what it means to be fully alive.

This is not an autobiography. Nor is it a memoir. I share these stories not to call attention to me, but to call attention to you. My intention is to get the party started – *your party* – a chance to take a look into the mirror of story and see, reflected back to you, parts of yourself that may have been hidden from view.

This is precisely why I have written this book. Rather than give in to the despair, despondency, and disillusionment that has become the world's default position these days, I've decided to do everything within my power to reclaim the collective narrative for the greater good – to revolve around a different sun – the one that lights up our lives from the inside. And it all begins with story.

You don't need to be an anthropologist to figure this out. Deconstruct any scripture, sermon, or TED talk and you will find *story*. That's how most meaningful messages are conveyed. Even the neuroscientists agree. When storytellers share their experiences, the same parts of the brain that light up in the storyteller upon telling their story, light up in the *listener* upon hearing it. This is called "mood contagion." "Somatic states." "Neural coupling" – the phenomenon of one person transmitting not only information about X, Y, or Z, but also the *experience itself.*

The question isn't whether or not storytelling works. It does. The question is: "Are we going to step up and tell our stories?"

Every day, when a friend passes you on the street and asks "Whassup?" you have a choice to make. You can talk about your aching back, the weather, or the latest political catastrophe, or you can elevate the conversation by telling a story that matters. All you need to do is be yourself, choose wisely, and seize the moment.

To help you make your way towards the frontlines of storytelling, in Part One I've included 40 stories for your inspiration and delight – 30 memorable "rock splitting moments" from my own life and 10 classic teaching tales, many of which have been told for centuries. A guiding question follows each story so you can apply the story's message to your own life. Part Two is a *Field Guide*, complete with tips, tools, and techniques for how you can become a better, more confident storyteller. Or, if you really want to go for it, how you can become a *storytelling revolutionary* on the frontlines of your own life –a sacred activist of insight, wisdom, and love.

Ready? I hope so. It's time to gather around the fire and begin...

PART ONE
The Stories

"There is no greater agony than bearing an untold story inside you."

– Maya Angelou

A SMALL BAG OF RED BERRIES

Today, sitting in Mesa Grande, the cafe I most love to frequent in San Miguel de Allende, I noticed an old, weathered woman entering the place. Dark-skinned, wrinkled, and small, she moved slowly across the room, more like shuffling than walking, stopping at each table and attempting to sell whatever it was she carried in her gnarled left hand.

Averting my eyes, I felt myself withdrawing, not wanting to encounter yet another beggar of the day needing something else to survive, but she kept coming, pausing now and then to rest.

When she finally made it to my table, she just stood there. That's it. She said nothing. She did nothing. She just stood there, holding in her left hand what appeared to be a bag of small red berries. I continued pretending to be busy, looking down, not wanting to be yet another refusal she would get that day, hoping she would leave so I could continue working, but she did not leave. She stood her ground like a thousand generations of *abuelas* before her who knew that they were here first.

Unable to ignore her any longer, I slowly raised my head, then drifted into her eyes. She held my gaze for a long time. Like a flower. Like the way a baby, unblinking, looks at a stranger. Gently, she shook her bag of berries once, explaining without a single word that she was not a beggar, simply a seller of small red berries on a Tuesday afternoon. In the distance, I heard the whooshing sound of a cappuccino machine.

"*Cuanto?*" I asked, holding her gaze.

"*Veinte,*" she replied.

"*Veinte?*" I asked again, wanting to stay with her for as long as my Spanish would allow.

"*Si,*" she said. "*Veinte.*"

"*Bueno,*" I replied, pulling a 20-peso note from my pocket and placing it in her small, brown hand. Smiling ever so slightly, she handed me the bag of berries, bowed, and continued on her way.

I checked my email. I made a list. I ate a piece of fruit. Ten minutes later, Carlos, the waiter, walked over to me, saw the bag of berries on the table and asked if he could have one.

"Si, Carlos," I said, opening the bag so he could choose his favorite.

An hour later, when it was time to pay the bill, I handed Carlos the bag and asked him to share the contents with his *esposa* and *hijo* when he got home that night. A few people came and went. Someone ordered a croissant. But Carlos and I just stood there, grinning, unmoving, a bag of small, red berries now the center of our world.

FOR YOUR REFLECTION:

Many of us hesitate to share our stories because we think they need to be earth shattering, cosmic, or worthy of a Hollywood screenplay. Sorry. Not true. Some of the most powerful stories are the so-called small ones. William Blake, the 16th century poet, advised us to "see eternity in a grain of sand." Henry Miller had his own spin on it: "The moment one gives close attention to anything, even a blade of grass, it becomes a mysterious, awesome, indescribably magnificent world in itself." Today, be on the lookout for small stories – "eternity in a grain of sand" moments – your version of my encounter with the berry-selling beggar. See what might be there for you. And if you're fortunate enough to have such a moment in time, share your story with a friend.

ON BEING VISITED BY AN ANGEL

Full disclosure: I have never been a person who believed in angels. Angels, to me, were merely poetic metaphors, the etheric embodiments of hard-to-describe feelings that some religiously-inclined people experienced when betwixt and between – some kind of fairy tale mix of loneliness, love, and longing for something beyond what their own two eyes could see. Hovering somewhere between God and the Easter Bunny, angels struck me as nothing more than projections, the astral version of what imaginative children have been inventing for centuries – "invisible friends."

This all changed for me one unforgettable night in 1974.

I was 27, two years into my first marriage, and all was not right with the world, at least not with *my* world. To most outside observers, my marriage looked just fine. We were a good-looking couple, had wonderful friends, great jobs in a children's hospital, and the same inspiring spiritual master. We grew lettuce, tomatoes, and watermelons in our garden, but, at the same time, we were growing further apart. The honeymoon was over, replaced by a strange brew of second thoughts, boredom, and judgment. My response to the situation, honed from many past lives as a monk? "Go within," a phrase I now understand was nothing more than my own DaVinci code for denial. My wife's response? Bake more bread. This gave us the appearance of having a home life – compensation for my not-so-subtle disappearing act.

Having a child, we thought, would fill the hole. And so we tried. But she had cysts on her ovaries and we were told it was not in the cards. So we settled into a childless marriage, skirting the edges of our life, and throwing ourselves into our work.

When she called me from LA at the end of a two-week business trip, I could tell by the sound of her voice that everything was just about to change. And so it did. She was having an affair with another man – someone who truly loved her, she explained, and was extending her trip for another three months.

"What? An affair? But what about us?" I managed to say – the kind of lines a Hollywood script doctor might read, poolside, and rewrite, ordering a second martini. But she had made up her mind. And that was that.

When I put down the phone, I was in shock. Stunned. Numb. Paralyzed. I couldn't move.

From that moment on, life started getting very strange for me. I'd stare at a wedding picture of the two of us on a wall and it would fall off. I'd have clairvoyant dreams of her lover. But even stranger, I'd find myself crying, in the middle of the day, in my car, for no apparent reason. Simply put, I was falling apart – a sad, lonely, guilty, depressed, embarrassed, disoriented young man too ashamed and self-loathing to share his private agony with even his best friend.

And so it continued for another three months.

And then, quite suddenly, on the night of the full moon in November, at the end of my ever-shortening rope, I decided to put an end to the madness. I picked up my meditation cushion, my meditation blanket, and a flashlight, exited my apartment, and walked into the forest that bordered my house. There, in a small clearing, I sat down, wrapped my blanket around my shoulders, closed my eyes, and started to meditate. My intention? To sit there, for however long it took, until I was free of the pain. I'm sure if someone, walking their dog, had passed by, it must have looked like a scene from Siddhartha, but on the *inside* it was a very different story. On the inside, a war was raging. And the battlefield was littered with the wounded, the dead, and at least a few deserters pretending to be dead so they wouldn't have to die. I just sat there. On that cushion. In the cold, experiencing, for the entire time, not even a second of peace. Nothing but a mind on fire. But I kept sitting. I had to. I had no other choice. There was nowhere else to go. There was nothing else to do. This was it. It had all come down this. Either *let go or lose my life*. Those were my choices.

And then, with absolutely no warning, no drumroll from beyond, my mind completely stopped. It. Stopped. Just. Like. That. The battle was over. The war ended. I wasn't just sitting in the clearing. I *was* the clearing. The pain that had ruled me those past few months had completely fallen away. The fever broke. If I had been a snake, my old skin would have fallen off. I, for the first time in what seemed like forever, was free. And so, I simply stood, walked back to my apartment, and went to bed. It was the first good night's sleep I'd had in months.

A few hours later, the phone ringing woke me up. My wife. "Mitchell," she began. "I feel horrible. I am so sorry for what I've done. I want to come home. Will you take me back? Will you forgive me?"

This is not at all what I wanted to hear. Less than six hours into my new life as a free man and now I was being asked to forgive her? Really? Just like that? On the phone? In my pajamas? After I had finally surrendered everything to begin my new life? A long silence followed. And a longer silence after that.

"Yes," I heard myself, saying. "Yes, I forgive you. Just get your flight times together and I'll pick you up at the airport."

Three days passed. I drove to the airport. I waited at the end of a long, tiled hallway. I scanned the faces of the many strangers getting off the plane. And then I saw her. She wore something new, a blue dress, and seemed to be happy. I wore something old and wasn't. We hugged, but nobody was home – two actors in a low-budget movie, the director shaking his head. The ride home? Icy cold, our nervous small talk a desperate attempt to fill the growing silence.

I don't remember what we had for dinner that night. I don't remember her unpacking. All I remember is getting into bed, my only desire to *sleep*. I laid my head on the pillow and closed my eyes. And then, I don't know why, I opened my eyes and standing in the middle of the room, I saw a radiant being of light – a glowing, translucent being of light, wings the color of moonlight folded into her sides. She just stood there looking at me. That was it. Just looking at me. And, I had never, in all my life, ever felt so cared for, so calm, and so sheltered from the storm.

"Oh, my God, I see an angel!" And, without a second thought, I fell immediately asleep.

In the morning, when I awoke, thoughts of the angel filled my head. *Did this really happen to me? Did I really see an angel? Or was it only a dream?* I turned to the woman, still my wife, and asked: "Did I… say something… last night… before I fell asleep?"

"Yes, you said, *'Oh my God I see an angel.'*"

The next day, looking for some much-needed inspiration, we made our way to a nearby bookstore – the spiritual kind. She went left and I went right, feeling totally guided, with no specific goal in mind. I walked to the back of the store, stopped, and looked up. I was standing in front of a section of books devoted entirely to angels. Taking a long, slow breath, I extended my hand and let it rest on the first book it touched.

I pulled it out. It was a book by Rudolf Steiner with a very memorable name: *On Angels*. I opened it randomly and began to read – a simple explanation of how everyone on planet Earth has a guardian angel, sometimes more than one, and that guardian angels make their appearance to human beings during times of great emotional turmoil for one purpose and one purpose only – to bring comfort, love, and protection. The time of day these angels make their appearance? The last few seconds before sleep or the first few seconds upon waking – the times when our analytical, rational mind is most at rest and a kind of portal opens to another realm.

I just stood there, book in hand, shaking, tears of joy streaming down my face.

FOR YOUR REFLECTION:

I have told this story to very few people in my life. Ruled by the assumption that I couldn't find the words and, even if I could, my words would only pervert the sacredness of my experience. So I chose to remain silent. But that time has passed. I realize now, as I move closer to the other side myself, that it is not only my duty to report what I have seen, but also my great pleasure. To any reader of mine who thinks that what I saw was self-invented, let me say this – what I saw that night, in my room, was as real as you are, if not more real. Indeed, if I saw you today and told someone *later* that I saw you, it is doubtful they would question my seeing you. How had I known it was you I was seeing and not my mind playing tricks? Good question, one we rarely ask. But with the sighting of an angel, questions rule the day. Doubts creep in. To the person who has seen the angel, nothing is subject to doubt and nothing needs explaining. Simply put, there's a time in all of our lives when something pierces the veil and we see the unseen. We become witnesses to the beyond. And so, I will leave you with this: *Angels* exist. I have seen one. One of them visited me in my bedroom at my time of greatest need. It said nothing. It did nothing. It just radiated the presence of love in a way that changed the way I experience life. I received the kind of love that made everything, now and forever, absolutely beautiful, meaningful, sacred, and whole.

What beyond human forces of love have made an appearance in your life? What hard-to-describe moment of divine intervention has touched you in some way? And is there anyone in your life who might benefit from hearing your story?

THE 18TH CAMEL

Many years ago, not far from the Great Sphinx, there lived a much beloved man named Hamid. Hamid was known throughout the land as the finest purveyor of camels in all of Egypt. He was not only an expert in every species of camel that had ever walked the earth, but he also treated everyone with kindness and compassion. So, when he fell off his camel one dark day in December and suddenly died, the entire nation mourned. It did not take long for word to spread that Hamid the Camel Merchant had left his mortal coil. Thousands of people found their way to his funeral to pay their last respects, perhaps the most lavish funeral ever to be witnessed in Egypt, more lavish, it has been said, than even the funerals of the pharaohs. Many high priests spoke. The finest of food was served and endless wine imbibed.

On the morning after the funeral, Hamid the Camel Merchant's Finance Minister, with great gravitas, called Hamid's three sons together for the ritual reading of the will. While greatly saddened by their father's demise, they were also greatly curious to find out what their illustrious father had bequeathed them. The reading of the will went on for hours, there being much to distribute, but it was the final piece of their inheritance, the last item read, that proved the most intriguing: Hamid's prize possession – his finest 17 camels. As his final instructions dictated, one half of his camels went to his eldest son, one third to the middle son, and one ninth to the youngest. The only problem? Seventeen camels cannot be divided in half. Nor can they be divided into thirds, or ninths.

And so when the Finance Minister completed the reading of the will, the three sons began arguing, each loudly making their case for how they thought their dearly departed father wanted his 17 favorite camels to be distributed. Soon their arguments turned to pushing and then to wrestling on the ground. Exhausted by their struggles, the three sons finally agreed to ask for help and sent word to the local wise man.

An hour later, the wise man arrived, asking each son to share his ideas for how this difficult matter might be resolved. Upon hearing the ideas of each son, the wise man stroked his beard, nodded, and smiled. Then, the wise man bowed and explained he would return in one hour with the solution.

An hour passed. And then, far off in the distance, midday sun shimmering off of the hot desert sand, they saw the wise man making his way towards them, riding on a camel.

"Most esteemed sons of Hamid," he began, upon dismounting his camel. "I have so much respect for your dearly departed father that it is my great pleasure today to donate one of my own camels to your inheritance. By my calculations, you now have 18 camels. Is that correct?"

The three sons nodded their heads in agreement.

"And so," continued the wise man, "now that you have 18 camels, I hereby bequeath half of them to the eldest – which, by my calculations, would be... let's see... *nine*."

Turning to the next son, the wise man continued. "And you, oh fine, upstanding middle son, are inheritor of one-third. So, by my calculations, you are to receive *six*."

Then, directing his attention to the remaining son, the wise man pronounced, "You, youngest son, are hereby awarded one-ninth of your father's camels. Let's see... one ninth of 18 equals *two*. And so, there you have it, your father's 17 prized camels fairly distributed. The eldest of you has received nine. The middle son, six, and the youngest son, two. 9 + 6 + 2 is 17, which, by my calculations, leaves one camel remaining. So I guess, now that your 17 camels have been fairly distributed, I'll just ride the 18th camel – *mine* – back to my home. Good day, oh grieving sons of Hamid, the Camel Merchant. May God shine his countenance upon you from this day forward."

FOR YOUR REFLECTION:

Some problems have an obvious solution. Some don't. But just because a problem doesn't have an obvious solution, doesn't mean no solution is forthcoming. Often, the most brilliant solutions are invisible at first blush and require a different kind of thinking. *What seemingly unsolvable problem of yours might require a different kind of approach than the one you are currently taking? Might there be a wise man or wise woman, nearby, whose counsel you might call on to hasten the appearance of an elegant solution?*

THE FLOWER FROM THE SKY

Be Here Now was the Bible of the 1960s or, if not the Bible, then at least the *Bhagavad Gita* – a book that bridged the gap between East and West for an entire generation of long-haired, counterculture, God-seeking souls. And I was one of them.

The author of the book, Baba Ram Dass, the ex-Harvard psychologist and popularizer (along with Timothy Leary) of LSD, was fast becoming a new kind of spiritual rock star. He had just returned from his pilgrimage to India with a ton of love and something far better than the Holy Grail: the ability to communicate the essence of Eastern wisdom in ways even suburban hippies could understand.

I read his book three times the first month I owned it. I read it twice the second month. So when I heard he was going to be speaking just a few miles from where I lived in Cambridge, Massachusetts, I bought a ticket and went.

The evening was divided into three parts: Part One was a kind of introduction – Ram Dass holding forth in ways even your mother would enjoy. He was charming. He was inspiring. And he made a lot of sense. An hour into his discourse, Ram Dass announced there was going to be an intermission and that if anyone really needed to leave, now would be a good time. And so some did.

Part Two went deeper. Much deeper. If Part One was Spirituality 101, Part Two was graduate school, complete with astounding stories about his guru, the blanket-wearing, Neem Karoli Baba. After an hour or so, he informed the audience there was going to be yet another break, the perfect time, he explained, for anyone to leave who had to get home for any reason. And so, another wave of people left, leaving about half of the original audience in the hall, the hard-core people who weren't going to leave until Ram Dass himself left or hell froze over, which ever came first.

Part Three went even deeper – a magical mystery tour into various nooks and crannies of the spiritual adventure all of us were on, no matter what path we walked. And then, as the midnight hour approached, with a sly smile and a slow bow, Ram Dass walked to the front of the stage, removed the garland of flowers that adorned his neck and, one by one, began tossing flowers into the audience, his gesture for recycling some of the love that had been directed his way all night. Immediately, mostly everyone stood and began reaching, Ram Dass continuing to toss.

When he turned in my direction, I had a decision to make. Do I stand and join the people standing all around me, or do I simply sit, cross-legged, where I was, hands on my knees in classic mudra position, thumb and index finger joined, palms upward to the sky?

Content as I was, free of need, I did not move. I just sat there, watching Ram Dass toss another flower. It was yellow and I could see it coming towards me, in slow motion, it seemed – a kind of time-lapse photography of my life. The closer it got, the more people reached for it, everyone wanting a memento of the evening. I continued sitting my ground. Looking up, it felt as if I was in a giant pinball machine, the many arms above me, all at different levels, flippers poised for action. The tallest person near me touched the flower, but, when he closed his hand, he missed and the flower continued its descent. A second person reached... and then a third, in a succession of seven – each failing to catch the object of their desire. I did nothing. I just sat there, watching, both of my hands open on my knees.

And then with absolutely no effort, not a millimeter of adjustment to the falling object, the flower landed perfectly in my right hand, bright yellow petals facing upward to the sky.

FOR YOUR REFFLECTION:

This little story happened to me 44 years ago, but it feels like yesterday because the lesson I learned was a timeless one. What kind of effort do I truly need to make in life? What does it take to achieve what I want? For most of my life, I have made a lot of effort, standing tall, reaching for what I wanted. Effort, I reasoned, is what it took to accomplish my goals. Who can argue with that? Read about the lives of anyone who has ever made a difference in the world and you will discover a tremendous amount of effort has been made. I get it. But there are times when the usual kind of effort that human beings make will not suffice, when trying and reaching and grasping get in the way. Ever try to catch a milkweed pod floating by? More often than not, the wind of your reaching pushes the milkweed further away. Bold reaching doesn't always work. Nor does grasping. Sometimes, we need to let things come to us. Sometimes, we need to strike the pose of *receiving* and trust the process of life. That's how the flower landed in my hand. And that's how the flower will land in *your* hand. Knowing when to sit and when to stand, of course, is something only you can decide. There is no formula. It's a moment-by-moment act of discovery. If you are experiencing, these days, that all of your standing and reaching and grasping is leaving you empty-handed, consider another approach. Slow down. Sit still. Open your eyes and your heart and your hands and let whatever you need come to you in its own sweet time.

MY FATHER'S LAST BREATH

There is a time of life when the time of life is about to end: the time of last breaths, the time of saying goodbye to everything you have ever known or loved, the time of letting go. This is the time in which my father now finds himself. He is flat on his back in a hospital bed, but the hospital bed is in his bedroom in West Palm Beach, which is where he has chosen to die – and will.

There will be no more calls to 911, no more paramedics, no more blood transfusions, no more needles, pills, or tests. This is his deathbed and we are around it, me, his son; his daughter, my sister; my wife, his daughter-in-law; grandchildren, great grandchildren, and the ever-present hospice nurse trying to keep him as comfortable as possible.

His mouth is dry. He cannot swallow. Someone swabs his lips as he gathers what's left of his strength to move his tongue toward the precious few drops of water. The soundtrack for his last night on Earth is an oxygen machine pumping purified air through transparent tubes clipped to the end of his nose. On the counter, creams. Creams for this and creams for that and creams for the other thing, too. I've never seen so many creams.

Those of us around his bed are very still, holding his hand, rubbing his back, looking at him and each other in ways we have never looked before.

There is very little for my father to do but breathe. This lion of a man whose life was defined by ferocity and action is barely moving now. A turn of the head. A flutter of the eye. A twitch. Though his eyes are closed, I know he can hear, so I bend closer and talk into his good, right ear. I tell him he's done a good job and that all of us will be OK. I tell him I love him and to go to the light. I tell him everything is fine and he can let go.

The hospice nurse is monitoring his vital signs. They keep getting lower and lower. I touch my father's cheek. It is cooler than before. His skin looks translucent, almost like a baby's. He opens his eyes and shuts them once again. None of us around him know what to do, but that's OK because it is very clear there is nothing to do.

Being is the only thing that's happening here.

My father had his last shot of morphine about an hour ago. He had his last bowl of Cheerios yesterday at 10 AM, Cheerios and half of a sliced banana. That was the last time he could swallow.

It is quiet in the room. Very quiet. I see my sister, my nieces, my wife, the nurse. All of us are as helpless as my father. The only difference is we are standing.

If only we could pay as much attention to the living as we do to the dying. If only we could stop long enough from whatever occupies our time and truly care for each other, aware of just how precious each breath is, each word, each touch, each glance.

Sitting by my father's side, I am hyperaware of everyone who enters the room, the way they approach his bed, what they say, how they say it, the look on their face, their thoughts. I want to be this conscious all the time, attuned to the impact I have on others in everything I do. It all matters. Nothing has prepared us for this moment. Not the books on death and dying, not the stories of friends whose fathers have gone before. Not the sage counsel of the Rabbi. Nothing.

One thing is clear. Each of us will get our turn. Our bodies, like rusty old cars gone beyond their warranties, will wear out. Friends and family will gather by our side, speak in hushed tones, hold our hands, and ask if we are comfortable. That's just the way it is. It begins with a breath, the first, and ends with a breath, the last. In between? A length of time. A span of years. A hyphen, as my teacher likes to say, between birth and death.

What this hyphenated experience will be is totally up to us. Will it be filled with kindness? Love? Compassion? Gratitude? Will we be there for each other before it's time to fill out the forms and watch the body, strapped to a stretcher by two men in black suits, driven away like something repossessed?

I hope so. I really do. I hope we all choose wisely. I hope beyond a shadow of a doubt that before we walk through the shadow of the valley of death that we choose to hold each others' hands NOW, rub each others' backs, bring each other tea, and listen from the heart with the same kind of infinite tenderness we too often reserve only for those about to depart.

My father is very quiet now, breathing only every 20 seconds or so. Or should I say being breathed? And then, there is nothing. Only silence. No breaths come. No slight changes of expression on his face. No whispered words of love. We, around his bed, are in his home, but he is somewhere else. Bye-bye Daddy! Travel well! Know we love you and will keep the flame of who you are deeply alive in our hearts. Thank you for everything. We will meet again. Amen!

FOR YOUR REFLECTION:

Common knowledge dictates that there are two things you can count on in life: death and taxes. I'd like to propose a third: *stories.* Indeed, I know people who don't pay taxes, but I don't know anyone who doesn't tell stories. But when you combine two of these three – *death and storytelling,* you get a very powerful combination – a combination with the power to cut through the hocus pocus of life into the heart of the matter. If you are reading this, there's a good chance that someone close to you has died: your mother, father, grandparents, child, or best friend. And there's also a good chance you have witnessed something profound in their passing, whether you were physically with them or not. Be willing to share that story with others! It is not ego to tell that story. On the contrary, it's the *dissolution* of ego – your opportunity to remind another person, without preaching, just how sacred each and every breath is. *What story of someone's death are you inspired to tell? And to whom?*

THE PATH IS MADE BY WALKING ON IT

Back in the late 1990s, in New York City, there lived a world-class architect who had just spent the last two years of his life designing and building what many people were claiming to be the best inner-city housing project ever constructed.

Although the world stood up and took notice, the architect's friends were totally baffled why a man of his stature would have taken on such a seemingly mundane project. After all, this was a man who had designed some of the world's finest museums. This was a man who had designed more than 20 celebrity mansions and a yacht club on the French Riviera. Why he had chosen to design an inner-city housing project was absolutely inconceivable to them.

But not to him. As the son of immigrant parents, he had grown up in a two-room, cold-water flat. His bedroom was actually the hallway. In college, he had to work two jobs to pay his tuition and in graduate school, three. Housing was always an issue for him – a mix of couch-surfing, rat-infested tenements, and ridiculously small studio apartments.

So when he heard about the inner-city housing project, his ears perked up. To him, this was an opportunity of a lifetime, a message from God, a chance to give back.

With great delight, he threw himself headlong into the project. It took every ounce of energy he had, what with the corrupt labor unions and the crazy New York politics, but he pressed on and, in 18 months, had created something so extraordinary that the press was calling it "The Taj Mahal of Inner-City Housing."

When the big day came to officially dedicate his creation, everyone was there – the Mayor, the Deputy Mayor, the Assistant to the Deputy Mayor, the Assistant to the Deputy Mayor's Assistant, his parents, wife, kids, therapist, and 500 housing project residents.

Wine was plentiful. So was the cheese and crackers. There was even a reggae band. The Mayor, as you might expect, spoke first. Then came the Deputy Mayor and the Head of the Tenant's Association. Finally, the architect spoke. At the end of his talk, he raised a magnum of champagne high over his head and, in the grand tradition of sea captains christening sailing vessels, smashed it on the corner of Building #1.

People cheered. Flashbulbs popped. Champagne guzzled. Everything was as upbeat as possible. That is, until the architect noticed a very large woman, in the back of the crowd, pacing back and forth. She did not clap. She did not cheer. She did not drink champagne.

"HEY!" she screamed at the top of her lungs. "Something is wrong here, very wrong." And with that, she began hurriedly making her way forward.

The architect, tapped his microphone, quieted the crowd, and invited her to join him on stage.

"Yes, my good woman," he began, "what seems to be the problem?"

"Please don't get me wrong, sir," she began, "I love what you've created here. And I love that I now have a beautiful home I can afford. But..."

"Yes?" the architect replied." But *what*?"

"But," she continued, with a dramatic sweep of her hand in the direction of the courtyard. *There are no sidewalks! Where are the sidewalks?* Millions of dollars have been spent on this place and I don't see a single sidewalk."

"Ah..." the architect replied, "a most astute observation, dear lady. Yes, you are absolutely right. There are no sidewalks. Not a single one. And do you know why?"

"No, I don't," she replied.

"There are no sidewalks, *because I don't yet know where people walk*. So, I've decided to wait a season, notice the paths people make when walking from building to building and *then* pave over them."

FOR YOUR REFLECTION:

In what ways does the architect's choice to wait a few months before adding sidewalks relate to a project of yours? *What patterns or feedback do you need to pay more attention to? Where might it be best to let things organically unfold rather than making an arbitrary decision that has no correlation to the real needs of the people you are serving? Where might* improv *be the path to improvement?*

WHAT I LEARNED FROM LISTENING TO RAVEL'S BOLERO

During the course of a lifetime a human being goes through many rites of passage. Birth, for example. First love. The death of a family member. Filing your taxes for the first time. For me, one of the most memorable rites of passage happened in college during my "pledge weekend" – the weekend I was initiated into a fraternity.

I realize, of course, especially in these politically correct times, that college fraternities are rarely associated with anything remotely smacking of insight, awareness, or transformation. But, for me, the rite-of-passage night that I was initiated into Pi Lambda Phi was an experience now permanently etched into whatever remains of my mind.

The initiation? To sit blindfolded in a pitch-black room, next to 21 of my sweating classmates, all of us holding 17 marbles in our left hands while listening to Ravel's "Bolero." That is not a misprint, folks. Fourteen hours of "Bolero." Fourteen.

If you are not familiar with "Bolero," allow me to briefly introduce it to you. It goes a little something like this: dahhhh, dah dah dah dah dah dah dah dah dah, dah, dah dah dahhhh, dah dah dah, dah dah dah dah dah dah dah dah dah dah dah dah dah.

It is, shall we say, an extremely repetitive piece of music, a kind of mental military mantra, one that requires the kind of refined, appreciative sensibility that none of us in that room possessed. I think the operational word here is *torture*, a kind of classical music waterboarding experience, from which I still have not yet completely recovered. Five minutes of "Bolero" is usually enough for most people. Fourteen hours is like the last year of a really bad marriage.

Now here's where it gets really interesting. By the grace of the "Bolero" gods and the fact that the recording we were listening to had been made on a reel-to-reel tape player, every 17 minutes or so there would be a four-second delay before the music looped back to the beginning. Four seconds. That was it. Every 17 minutes we had a four-second reprieve from Mrs. Ravel's lunatic son.

What I learned during those four seconds taught me a lesson I will never forget.

Those four seconds were not memorable because of the sudden silence in that darkened room, but because of what happened during the silence, the space that opened up, a chance for the 22 of us to enjoy a blast of divine humor – humor initiated by the youngest of us in the room that day, the Honorable Barry "Spunky Boonbeam" Birnbaum (now a much sought after attorney in New York City). What Barry did during those precious few seconds not only renewed and refreshed us, it most likely prevented the lot of us from spending the rest of our lives in a loony bin.

"Nice beat, but you can't dance to it," Barry commented during the first of our four- second reprieves. "More bass! More bass!" he announced the second time around. "I much prefer the London Philharmonic version," he interjected after round three. And so on it went, 49 times every 17 minutes throughout that dark night of our collective soul.

The laughter that followed Barry's comments refreshed our minds and rebooted our souls. Humor saved the day. Humor gave us new life. Or as Gandhi once confessed, "If I had no sense of humor I would long ago have committed suicide."

FOR YOUR REFLECTION:

Humor is the great equalizer, no matter who you are and what you do. It opens the heart, relaxes the mind, defuses worry, energizes, uplifts, renews, restores, and rejuvenates. I like to think of it as one of the core universal truths on planet Earth. *Beyond* this earth, I cannot say for sure, other than my current perception that ETs, at least in the pictures I've seen of them, never seem to be smiling. I don't get it. They are all so serious. All that advanced consciousness and still no sense of humor. Really? REALLY? I have no idea if extraterrestrials listen to "Bolero" or think George Carlin is funny, but I do know this: humor is a gift from God. Humor is divine. Humor is wisdom wearing a smile. *Why else do you think the court jesters had the ear of the King?*

A VERY UNEXPECTED JOURNEY

Yesterday was a very off-the-grid day for me. It began as most of my days do here in San Miguel de Allende. I slept until I wasn't tired. I meditated. Then I checked my email. Upon noticing the internet was down, I got the keys to my out-of-town neighbor's apartment, let myself in, booted up my Mac, and logged onto a webinar I very much wanted to attend.

So far, so good. The sun was shining. Donald Trump was not yet President. And to my left, wrapped in silver foil, I saw something that looked like gum, so I opened it up and, seeing that it wasn't gum, but a small bar of chocolate, broke off two pieces, and wolfed them down.

The webinar, all about the phenomenon of "collective narrative," captivated me, so instead of playing the role of passive webinar participant, I decided to accept the moderator's invitation to enter my comments in the chat box.

"The world is an illusion, but you have to act as if it's real," I wrote, quoting Krishna.

The webinar presenter, savvy business consultant, Peter Block, seemed almost Zen Master-like in his demeanor. Deep. Sagacious. And astoundingly precise. The more I listened, the more inspired I got, almost as if I was on the receiving end of some kind of cosmic transmission — what spiritually-minded people would call "shakti."

Wow. I loved this webinar! Totally fascinated and feeling a sudden need to stretch, I entered into a series of standing yoga positions that looked nothing like the ones in the books I'd bought, but never read. Webinar over, I began packing up my stuff, but the process of packing seemed to be taking a very long time.

"Hmmm", I thought to myself, "maybe this had something to do with me trying to process all of the cool wisdom about storytelling that had just been shared with me."

Possible? Sure, why not? Who knows how the mind works and how it affects the body. Yes, I was moving more slowly than usual. And yes, I was feeling light-headed, but hey, I lived in a mountain town that's 6,000 feet above sea level! I was not getting my usual dose of oxygen. Strange. I felt strange – kind of like nothing mattered and everything mattered at the exact same time.

Once home, I entered the kitchen and began talking to Evelyne, my dear, sweet, wife, who mentioned that I seemed to be "in a very different place than she was."

"Are you OK?" she asked, a look of concern in her eyes.

"OK?" I responded. "I am more than OK. *I am divine.*"

Yes, I was talking. That I was sure of. But my syntax and pacing were off, almost as if I was translating a Dead Sea Scroll in a language I didn't quite understand. Feeling a need to lie down, I found my way to the bedroom, turned on some music, and flopped down on the bed. All of a sudden it dawned on me that my light-headedness had nothing at all to do with the thin mountain air and must be health-related, the slow motion onset of a heart attack – you know, what happens to men my age who haven't had their cholesterol checked in a while.

"Great!" I thought. "I'm going to have a heart attack in Mexico. Who knows if they'll even accept my health insurance?"

The good news? Panic had not yet taken hold of me. No, I was far more curious than fearful, curious to discover if I had the power to neutralize the onsite of a heart attack through the skillful use of my mind. So I... slowed... my... breathing down... way down... the kind of down I imagined cave-dwelling yogis do when they hibernate for the winter. It worked! The heart attack stopped. I was just feeling good. Really good.

About this time, Evelyne informed me that I absolutely needed to take our neighbor's dog out for a walk and pick up the laundry three blocks away. While her request seemed poorly timed, I realized that, earlier in the day, I had promised and, being a man of my word, decided to follow through. Stuffing some pesos into my pocket, I walked downstairs, fetched the dog, and began the three-block trek to my local lavandaria.

As I walked the back streets of San Miguel, it soon became obvious that my gait had a bit of a stumbling quality to it. I wasn't so much walking as meandering. Yes, technically speaking, I was moving forward, but not directly forward, an experience I realized was not all that uncommon in beautiful San Miguel, what with the cobblestone streets and so much beauty to distract you. So I let that thought go, but then another took its place, a now very familiar thought, the heart attack thought – the same one I'd had just minutes before in my light-filled apartment.

Could it be? Was this really happening to me? Was I just about to die? Passing out on the street, near the intersection of Refugio and Vergel, would not be a good thing. First of all, I had no clue how to say "Excuse me, I am having a heart attack. Please take me to the nearest hospital." And secondly, I didn't want to worry Evelyne.

Clear that dying of a heart attack was not a good idea, I immediately returned to my earlier mind-over-matter practice and simply gathered my centrifugal energy. Bingo! It worked again like a charm. Suddenly, the heart attack passed. On the contrary, I was having some kind of spontaneously occurring spiritual experience – an unexpected opening of my kundalini, I think, or my chakras, or whatever happens on the inner planes when someone becomes fully awakened.

Possible? For sure. Why not? Indeed, I had often read about this kind of unexpected infusion of mystical power – much like the New Jersey housewife, years ago, who channeled enlightened souls from the great beyond, or Meher Baba, one of my early teachers, whose own teacher once hit him in between the eyes with a rock, causing him to wander around India for weeks, totally out of his mind.

"God intoxicated" was the phrase used to describe him. "Ecstatic."

Might this be the state of consciousness I had unexpectedly entered into? I mean, really, I was blissed out of my tree, in a state of pure being, a realm I might never return from – most likely, my new normal – a realm of existence that would clearly require some integration on my part.

Flashing on my list of undone tasks for the day, I remembered I had a conference call coming up with a prospective client from a large corporation – a call to explore my ideas for how I could help 1,400 of their tax auditors, in just 70 minutes, become more innovative.

As I announced this to Evelyne, upon my return, she was not, shall we say, confident I was in the right frame of mind for such communication. Always the optimist, I assured her I was fine and proceeded to lie down on the bed to organize my thinking. Ninja-like, I started writing notes on a yellow legal pad, three pages worth, very little of which I could read, when I realized that the real point I wanted to make on the call was not a point at all, but a question – perhaps, even, THE question: *What do you want to create?*

I mean, really, if a multi-billion dollar organization wanted me to have some kind of impact on 1,400 of their tax auditors in just 70 minutes, it sure seemed important that I understood what outcome they were looking for. Right? So I jotted down my question, dialed the number, and proceeded to have an extremely lucid 30-minute call with two women from the financial services industry who, it seemed, were becoming increasingly intrigued with what I had to say – so much so, in fact, that they asked me to submit a detailed proposal by the end of business day on the coming Friday.

It was 3:30 PM when the call ended. Remembering that Evelyne and I had guests coming for dinner in three hours, I began rallying my troops, some of whom had definitely deserted. I washed some dishes. I set the table. I found my stuff and cleaned it up.

I thoroughly enjoyed the dinner. And the conversation, too! Everyone took turns telling jokes and stories. And then, about 45 minutes into the meal, my downstairs neighbor, having just returned from his day trip and wanting to thank us for taking care of his dog, walked into the kitchen and started talking to Evelyne. I could hear loud laughter. Much loud laughter. Borderline hysterical laughter.

Then they both appeared in the dining room.

"How was the chocolate?" my neighbor asked. "Did you like it?"

A great silence filled the room. Ahhh.... NOW I understood! The chocolate I had eaten six hours ago was not your average piece of Mexican chocolate. It was of the "medicinal" variety – and the amount I had eaten was more than enough for two people. Cosmic shakti coming through my laptop? No. Slow motion heart attack? Not quite. Spontaneous spiritual transmission from the great beyond? Not today. Just me and the affects of a whole lotta THC.

For Your Reflection:

One of the big takeaways for me, from my chocolate-imbibing day, was just how addicted I am to making sense out of things. Something *happens* and I immediately interpret that something until it takes the shape of a story, me not necessarily realizing that the story I am telling is nothing more than my curious way of stringing together a few unrelated data points until it is believable. That's what the first sailors used to do. They looked up in the sky and drew lines between stars that were light years away from each other until their "connect the dots" moment resulted in a recognizable shape that they then proceeded to name and tell stories about to the next generation. The *real* story that's going on here, folks, the story behind the story, is the story of how you, me, and the other 7.6 billion people on planet Earth are making stuff up all the time and convincing ourselves (and others) that it's true. *Today, just experience life.* Don't make up any stories about it. Don't come to any conclusions. Just enjoy each story-free moment.

ENDING VIOLENCE WITH CHOPSTICKS

Once upon a time there was an old man sitting at a sushi bar in Japan, his back turned to the front door. Halfway through his meal, in walks three young thugs, with only one thing in mind – to attack the old man from behind and steal his money. Quickly looking around the room, they knew this would be an easy day's pay for them, since the old man was the only person in the restaurant. What they *didn't* know was that the old man was actually a great martial arts Master, a legend in self-defense, who had been trained from an early age to sense danger from behind.

As the three young thugs approached, the old man, lightly holding a pair of chopsticks in his right hand, plucked a housefly from the air. The young thugs noticed, their forward advance slowing. Then the martial arts Master transferred the chopsticks to his left hand, quickly flicked his wrist above his head, and caught a second housefly. The young thugs noticed again. Now, transferring the chopsticks to his right hand, the martial arts Master performed the feat again, plucking yet another housefly from the air and depositing it gently next to the other two, both of which were dazed, but very much alive. That's when the three young thugs stopped, turned around, and exited the restaurant. It took them 30 minutes before they could speak.

FOR YOUR REFLECTION:

I first heard this story from a sixth-degree black belt from the same martial arts tradition as the great Master sitting at the sushi bar. The story made a great impact on me, helping me understand how violence can be ended *without* violence and how mastery can manifest itself in many ways to accomplish an extraordinary result. "A good horse runs at the shadow of the whip," I believe the old saying goes. I always wanted to include the story in this book, but before publishing it, I needed to make sure I had it right, so I decided to do some research. I Googled. I emailed. I spoke to people from the Master's martial art's lineage. But every effort I made came up empty. Nobody could tell me, for sure, whether the story was true or not. That's when I realized I had a choice to make. Do I include the story in this book even though I don't have undeniable proof that it's true? Obviously, I have – and why I have is because of the powerful message it delivers. *In just two paragraphs that take only 90 seconds to read.* Did the story really happen the way I describe it? Maybe. Maybe not. I still don't know. But what I do know is there is a deep message embedded in the story – a message that, if deeply imbibed, has the potential to change the way you approach the perceived problems in your life.

Is any story 100% factual? And, other than a story being told in a court of law, does it really matter? Stories, by their very nature, morph in the telling. They also morph in relationship to the storyteller's perceptions, interpretation, and mood of the moment –not unlike what happens in the children's game of Telephone. Facts are one thing. Truth is another. Maybe that's why Francis Bacon once said, "Truth is so hard to tell, it sometimes needs fiction to make it plausible."

What danger is approaching you these days? And how might you defuse it in a non-traditional way?

THE MAN FROM CROATIA

On a bold, cold night in January, two hours after my wife and children had gone to bed, I found myself sitting alone in my man cave, with nothing but a laptop, an iPhone, and the painful recognition that even though I had written five books, created a successful company, and had supported my family, in style, for 15 years, I had yet to accomplish a single meaningful thing in my life. This is a feeling writers know all too well, the moon howling moment of insight that their early promise of genius had either not borne fruit or the fruit was rotting in a bowl of an unhungry stranger many miles away. The kind of feeling, I imagined, at least partially responsible for Vincent Van Gogh cutting off his ear – a man who had sold but a single painting in his life, and to his brother, at that – a man who Vincent knew had bought his work mostly out of pity.

It was at precisely at this moment, too late to be early and too early to be late, when I glanced down at my laptop and noticed an email coming in from someone I didn't know, a man with very few vowels in his name. Clearly, this was not a friend. No. This was from a stranger, a man, he explained, from Croatia, who had been reading my blog for the past five years and now that he had been diagnosed with a terminal disease and had, at best, maybe three months to live, wanted me know that last night's posting had touched him in a way that filled him with gratitude. An oasis, it was, for him, he continued, a place to rest and let go of his pain. He was writing to me, he explained, to thank me and request that no matter what happened in my life – or didn't happen – *I should continue writing.*

FOR YOUR REFLECTION:

Think of a way you attempt to express yourself in this life – perhaps an effort that leaves you feeling like you haven't really succeeded? Got it? Good. Now think of a person who has benefitted from your expression. *Who is it? And how did your effort to express yourself benefit this person in some way?*

THE DANCE OF THE GNATS

The first time I was ever under the influence of a mind-altering substance, I spent the better part of the day in a Pennsylvania cornfield. After an unspecified amount of time adjusting to what was rapidly dawning on me to be an entirely different reality than the one I was accustomed to, I decided to lie down and, perhaps, for the first time in my life, have absolutely nothing to do.

This was the first time I had ever laid down in a Pennsylvania cornfield and I had no idea that the act of doing so was going to create the illusion that I was now six feet underground, having flattened the cornstalks beneath me with my sudden need to be prone. This was my first experience of being dead or, if not dead, per se, than at least dying, buried in a coffin, the lid not yet closed. I could see nothing but the blue sky overhead, a few clouds, and now, appearing from who knows where, a gigantic swarm of gnats not more than three inches from my face.

"Bugs!" my mind screamed. "BUGS!"

My right hand, which had been casually resting at my side just seconds before, now entered into a state of panic, its fingers preparing to swat. There is no way in the world I wanted to be attacked by a swarm of gnats here in this peaceful Pennsylvania cornfield. One swat, I was sure, was all it would take. Just one swat and I would be free of the danger. The swarm of gnats wouldn't have a chance. But something stayed my hand. Something would not allow me to strike, only observe, and then become totally fascinated by what I was seeing. There, before my eyes, just a few inches from the tip of my nose, hundreds of gnats were dancing. Their movements, repeated over and over and over again, formed what seemed to be some kind of divine crystal in space – a glowing, multi-sided geometric shape of unbelievable intricacy and radiance. Not a single gnat left formation. Not one. They just kept dancing, each one knowing their place, repeating the pattern over and over again. No gnats attacked me. Not once was I bothered or bitten. Only one thing was happening – the dance of the gnats here in this Pennsylvania cornfield. And all for an audience of one. Me.

For Your Reflection:

What is right before your eyes, these days, that you are getting ready to swat – something uninvited and potentially bothersome that might actually be some kind of divine message for you, a gift to be enjoyed? *What do you think the value of this uninvited "thing" might be?*

THE ECSTATIC RABBI

I am Jewish. My parents were Jewish. My grandparents were Jewish and all their parents and grandparents were Jewish. My father's father's name was Abraham. His father's name was Moses. I was circumcised, bar mitzvahed, and ate more than my share of bagels and lox. Like any good Jew, I celebrated the High Holidays.

Wait… hold on a minute… I don't think "celebrate" is actually the right word. Make that "endure" – me, as a young boy, being far more devoted to baseball and playing with my dog than fiddling around with that silky, red prayer-book marker separating one section of indecipherable Old Testament text from another.

My rabbi, the very forthright, wise, benevolent, Rabbi Alvin D. Rubin, always seemed, at least from my adolescent point of view, to be wondering if he had, somehow, lifetimes ago, taken a wrong turn out of the Sinai desert, finding himself, as he was, shepherding a flock of polyester-wearing suburbanites way more interested in their golf game than the unpronounceable name of God.

These were my roots, not the grey roots my canasta-playing mother religiously turned blond the day before each family visit to the temple, but roots nonetheless. The hand I was dealt. My karma. The surreal, slightly salty smorgasbord of my not-yet-enlightened life.

Please don't get me wrong. I am not complaining. My introduction to Judaism was not a bad experience. On the contrary, it was good – full of warmth, comfort, and the safety that comes from hanging out with one's own. But the older I got, the more it dawned on me that it wasn't religion I was looking for, but rather whatever it was that inspired religion to come into being in the first place – not the Ten Commandments, but the feeling of amazement that preceded them being inscribed on stone tablets.

And so, on the day I went off to college, I decided to take a break from Judaism. Though I still found the word Deuteronomy intriguing and knew, in my heart of hearts, I would miss the rugala after each irregularly attended Sabbath service, it was time for some new adventures.

Fast forward seven semesters to my senior year of college.

As I crossed the threshold into my parent's house for Christmas vacation (notice I didn't say "Hanukkah"), my mother greeted me with three words I will never forget: "The rabbi called" – a phrase that could only mean one thing: I had done something terribly wrong.

"He wants to see you," she continued, "tomorrow morning."

While not quite a burning-bush moment, I was definitely feeling the heat, as the echoes of my mother's words fanned out into the vast suburban horizon: "The rabbi wants to see you… The rabbi wants to see you… The rabbi wants to see you."

Though I hadn't been to temple for five years, I still remembered where it was and made my way there, dutifully, the next morning. Nervous? Yes. But more than that, curious. The Rabbi sat behind his desk, smiling, many, many books behind him.

"Mitchell", he said. "Welcome. I'm going to cut to the chase. We've been following your progress for years and, well, you see, there is shortage of Reform rabbis and I want you to seriously consider entering the Rabbinate."

The rest of our conversation suddenly blurred, me half Dustin Hoffman in *The Graduate* and half Lenny Bruce on speed. The Rabbi mentioned something about me not having to pay taxes on my future house and I mentioned something about a motorcycle.

Later that night, my father, whose belief in God seemed to be escalating exponentially the closer I got to losing my Vietnam-phobic college deferment, wanted to talk.

"How'd it go?" he asked. "What did the rabbi have to say?"

"Umm," I replied, stalling for time. "It was... interesting. The rabbi wants me to become a rabbi."

"That's great," my father blurted. "You'll make a great rabbi."

"But Dad," I said, "I don't believe in God."

My father looked up. "That's not so important," he said. "You like people, right? You like to read, right? You'll make a great rabbi."

"Umm. Dad... I don't think it works that way."

Five years passed. I went to graduate school (in poetry, not medicine). I married a shiksa (not a Jew). I took LSD (not the law boards). And I, blissfully, became the student of a 13-year old guru from India. My parent's response? A kind of dark night of the upper-middle-class Jewish soul punctuated with words like "tsuris," "meshugganah," and lots of other Yiddish words they used whenever they didn't want "the kids" to know what they were talking about.

But then a funny thing happened. The plot twisted. My good friend, Steven Ornstein, also Jewish and also a student of the same young, Indian guru, invited me to an "Evening with Shlomo Carlebach," a Jewish rabbi, and one of the leading lights of the Baal Teshuva movement – apparently designed to attract secular Jewish youth back into the fold. Shlomo, Steven assured me, was the real deal – not your run-of-the-mill rabbi, but a true keeper of the Jewish flame. So I went.

The first few minutes of Shlomo's presentation were unremarkable. What I saw was a disheveled man, with a beard and a guitar, mumbling a few words of introduction to a very conservative audience wearing their Sabbath best. First he started strumming. Then he started singing. Then he started smiling as if the Red Sea were about to part.

"OK, fine," I said to myself. "We're in for a Yiddish Hootenanny with a non-traditional rabbi just back from Israel. Cool."

But the next thing I knew, Shlomo was jumping up and down. Not just a little. A lot. This was not shtick. This was not some Borscht Belt Vegas act. This was a man plugged in, on fire, and all of us could feel the heat. With each deeply moving song he sang, Shlomo became more animated, more out there, but the "out there" he got wasn't out there at all. It was *in there*.

Something was going on inside this man and we could all sense it. His own promised land? It's hard to tell, but what wasn't hard to tell was how much he enjoyed himself and, even more than that, how much he wanted the rest of us to join in.

It's clear now, that Reb Shlomo Carlebach, wide-eyed, soulful leader of the still-forming Jewish renewal movement, was polarizing the room. Half of the congregation was with him. The other half was squirming in their seats, planning their escape. But Shlomo didn't mind. Like some kind of crazed bar mitzvah band leader in a parallel universe, he made a few gestures and got everyone standing, holding hands, and moving, in unison, up on stage and then down again, a curious mix of hora and suburban conga line.

I had never seen anything like this before in a temple. Never. We weren't praying, we were *playing* – the kind of play that had the power to spark the experience that prayer was supposed to ignite. Freedom. Joy. And gratitude. The last time I had been on a stage in a temple I was reciting my Haft Torah, 14 lines I had painstakingly memorized for months so I could "become a man." Now it was all improv. Nothing was rehearsed. Nothing was memorized. Nothing was at stake. The only thing happening was joy.

Shlomo walked to the ark, opened it, and took out the Torah. "Wait! Isn't that only supposed to happen on the High Holidays?" I thought. Apparently, Shlomo had just declared tonight to be one as he handed the Torah to whoever was closest to him and continued holding forth, hugging anyone he could get his hands on.

"My Holy Brother," he called to the young man to my left. "My Holy Brother, it is so good to be with you. My Holy Sister," he intoned to the woman standing to my right. "Do you know what a blessing you are on this Earth?"

And the amazing thing? Just by saying what he did it became instantly true. Whoever he hugged, whoever he directed his spontaneous declarations of love to suddenly felt holy, blessed, and totally alive – touched by the kind of "Lo, I say unto you" energy that has the power to instantly turn words into reality.

And then, with no absolute warning, he turned to me. "Oh my Holy Brother, " he exclaimed, tapping his mic, "go find the rabbi and tell him I need more power!"

Man on a mission, I descended the stage and began my search for the rabbi. It didn't take long. I found him in the kitchen, with his wife, putting on his overcoat. Rapidly. If this had been the Wild West, the rabbi was most definitely in his get-out-of-Dodge mode.

"Rabbi," I asked, with as much respect as I could muster. "Shlomo needs more power."

The rabbi said nothing. He just stood there, looking at me, shaking his head. The next thing I knew, he was out the door, his wife trailing behind him.

I returned to the main room. "Shlomo!" I exclaimed, "the Rabbi has left the building. He wasn't willing to give you any more power."

"Fine, my Holy Brother," he said. "I have my *own!*"

And with that, he unplugged the mic and began singing even louder than before, his jumping up and down some kind of unhinged call to prayer to anyone in the general vicinity.

Five minutes passed. Many people left. Those who stayed were all on stage, spinning in circles, laughing, singing, arms outstretched, or simply gazing into a distance becoming increasingly closer.

"Shlomo!" called a bearded young man in front of me, his shirt untucked. "Let's take this to my apartment! I live only two miles away."

And so the evening's caravan of love continued out the door, into cars, down a road, up some stairs, and into a book-lined, dimly lit abode of a local Hassid now kvelling, beyond belief, that Shlomo – Reb Shlomo Carlebach – charismatic, rule-breaking, wide-eyed leader of the still forming Jewish renewal movement, not having slept in God knows how long, was going to be holding forth (and fifth and sixth, no doubt) in just a few minutes, without a break, without a nap, and without a single complaint – a motley crew of Hassids, hippies, and holy fools by his side.

Standing next to my Holy Brother, Steven, in the middle of what no one had a name for, I have zero clues about what the protocols were, or if any existed, or why I'm even thinking at all. Shlomo certainly wasn't. He was just taking his seat – the one he was offered – while surveying the room and sensing, once again, that this HOLY MOMENT was the perfect time for a story. And so he began.

I remember nothing about the story he told that night, not the plot, not the setting, not the message. All I remember is the *feeling* – the feeling of wonder, the feeling of awe, the feeling of being absolutely in the right place at the right time and being so utterly glad to be alive.

And when he finished, which, by the way, he never was, a great laughter filled the room, followed by a flood of Talmudic references I had no clue about, and the voice of someone, from the back, called out, "That reminds me of a story, Reb Shlomo."

And so another one began... and then another... and then another, waves of spoken love and wisdom bubbling up from a very buoyant ocean we were all then swimming in.

But even ecstatic rabbis get tired, and Shlomo certainly was, his nodding no longer a sign of his off-the-grid appreciation of life, but a prelude to sleep, which was precisely when Steven and I approached and asked if he would like a ride back to his hotel.

Wired as this man was to the experience that everything was coming to him directly from God, he nodded, stood, and, as he exited the room with us by his side, embraced as many people as he could, said something kind to everyone – then continued with us, out the door, to the street below.

Thirty minutes later, we were in his hotel room, Shlomo making a beeline to a small bag of tangerines he had just brought back from Tel Aviv.

"These, my Holy Brothers, are so sweet. You must have one. You must." And with that, he began peeling, one for Steven and one for me.

The three of us sat silently on his rumpled bed enacting a Jewish ritual that transcends space and time – *noshing*, the enthusiastic chowing down of something yummy in between meals. Sweet. The tangerines were sweet. Very sweet.

Then Steven spoke. "Reb Shlomo," he began, "a few years ago, my friend Mitchell and I met a young Indian Master and received a very powerful inner experience called Knowledge. We are wondering if any of the Jewish holy books refer to such an experience."

Shlomo's ears perked up and his eyebrows arched, a signal to Steven to elaborate.

"Oh yes, YES!" he said. *"Absolutely,"* quoting from the Talmud, Kabbalah, and God knows how many other sacred texts.

Steven and I kept looking at each other. We could not believe our good fortune. I mean, there we were, completely out of the blue, having a private audience with Rabbi Shlomo Carlebach, wise man, spiritual genius, and storyteller supreme – when we noticed the room had suddenly become quiet. Very quiet. Curious, we both glanced at Shlomo. He was fast asleep, sprawled sideways on the bed like some kind of beached Biblical whale, snoring, shoes still on.

Steven, God knows why, leaned closer and whispered into Shlomo's ear the news that I was getting married in three weeks.

Shlomo sat bolt upright from a deep sleep. "I will perform the ceremony!" he exclaimed. "Yes! Me!"

If I had been Saul on a horse, I would have been knocked halfway to Cleveland, but I was not Saul on a horse. It was just me, Mitchell Lewis Ditkoff, sitting there on a bed with Shlomo Carlebach and my good buddy, Steven Ornstein, in a Boston hotel room, 5,504 miles from Jerusalem.

"Um…Shlomo," I said. "We… already have a rabbi."

His eyes open wider. "Is he… straight?"

"Well, Shlomo. He's a lot straighter than you."

And with that, Shlomo closed his eyes, leaned back, and fell fast asleep. Steven and I stood, turned out the light, and exited, laughing all the way home.

FOR YOUR REFLECTION:

Most human beings have been born into a religion, culture, or philosophy – a way of life inherited from their parents. Some of these human beings (me, included), in an attempt to become their "own person," end up rejecting most, if not all, of the givens they were born into. It's totally normal, rooted in our psychological need to individuate. The down side, unfortunately, is that we often end up throwing the baby out with the bathwater. My meeting with Reb Shlomo Carlbach revealed this to me in spades. My question for you? *What aspects of the life you were born into might you have rejected only because you were rebelling against your parents? Just for fun, choose one of these aspects and contemplate what unopened gifts might be waiting there for you.*

THE FINGER SNAP

Two years ago, I travelled from Woodstock to Malibu to work for a few days with my teacher, Prem Rawat, on a project he was very passionate about – the launch of his new enterprise, RawatCreations. More specifically, he wanted me to write about his approach to photography and the five photos he wanted to feature on his website.

The first of our meetings went well. We spent an hour talking about photography, his early boyhood fascination for it, the conditions necessary for high-level results, and his nuanced creative process. Later that night, I wrote what I thought was a pretty good description of the ground we covered, and emailed it, fingers crossed, to his secretary.

The next morning she called me to deliver his feedback. "More spices," was the message, the implication being that my writing was too bland.

So I got busy for another few hours and generated version 2.0. This draft, I thought, exceeded the quality of the first one – better organized, more accurate, and with just the right amount of spices. Happy to have accomplished my goal, I submitted my writing to Prem's secretary one more time.

A day passed. I went for a long walk. I reread what I had written five times. Then I got another call from his secretary, asking me to meet with him later that afternoon, an invitation that quickly revealed the two sides of my psyche. The first? "Wow! I get to spend time with my favorite person in the whole world." The second? "Oops! I probably screwed up royally!"

When Prem walked into the room, none of these thoughts were apparent. He was, as far as I could tell, completely present, happy, radiant, and ready to dive in once again, holding a copy of my most recent draft in his right hand.

"I'm not going to give you any rules," he explained, scanning my words and suggesting a few approaches to the writing I hadn't yet considered. To me, it felt like psychic surgery – him deftly reaching into my last draft and pointing out what needed to go. After a few minutes of elaboration, he stood, turned, and began to exit the room. As he did, I heard these words come blurting of my mouth: "So… it looks like I'll be up late tonight working on the third draft."

That's when he turned to me and snapped his fingers.

"You mean," I said, "this is supposed to be *easy*?"

He snapped his fingers again. Then I snapped mine. Then he snapped his. Four finger snaps. That was it. Then he pivoted and left the room.

Thirty minutes later I sat down to write again, but this time the writing flowed much easier than before and the quality was recognizably higher. While I knew my task mattered, I also knew that the main effort I needed to make was to *be in the moment and trust what I knew.*

Three years have passed since that day. My finger snapping moment with Prem Rawat continues to uplift and clarify every aspect of my life. In a way, it feels like a sacred seed has been watered in me, a seed of awareness now growing from the inside out – a seed that infuses all of my choices, especially the stuff I assume to be "difficult," with ease, simplicity, and grace.

FOR YOUR REFLECTION:

What project of yours, these days, gives you the impression that it will be difficult and a lot of work? *In what ways, might you simplify your approach and get the results you are seeking with less stress, drama, and struggle?*

THE BEST ARCHER IN ALL OF CHINA

Once upon a time there was a man named Wu Li, a most gifted archer. Time and again, Wu Li would enter archery tournaments and win. He won so often and so convincingly that word of his accomplishments soon spread throughout the land. By the time he turned 22, Wu Li was known as the best archer in all of China.

One day, upon returning home from yet another victory, Wu Li found himself rushing through a marketplace and bumping into an old man carrying a basket of potatoes. Potatoes went flying everywhere and the old man fell to the ground with a thud.

"Old man!" shouted Wu Li, "Get out of my way! Don't you know who I am?"

The old man looked up, squinting.

"Oh yes. I know who you are," he replied. "You are Wu Li, second best archer in all of China."

"Second best?" bellowed the gifted one. "Second? Ha! I am the best. There is no one in the world better than me."

The old man smiled and stood as he slowly gathered his potatoes.

"Yes, you are great, Wu Lei. But there is someone even greater than you!"

Wu Lei said nothing, his whole body poised like an arrow ready to launch.

"Who is this impostor? Where does he live?"

"Oh," the old man said slowly, as if entering a temple. "His name is Master Po. He lives many miles to the North, high atop Mount Chi Han."

"Then I will go and challenge him!" the archer exclaimed. "I will put an end to such nonsense."

Pushing past the old man, Wu Li stormed off into the night. For 30 days and nights he journeyed. When he finally arrived at the foot of the mountain, the young archer could not believe his eyes. The mountain was sheer rock face, covered with ice, and pitched at a 90-degree angle straight up to the sky, hidden by clouds. A lesser man would have ended his journey then and there. But not Wu Li. He climbed. And when he was done climbing, he climbed some more.

On the fourth day of his ascent, Wu Li saw the crest, grabbed onto a ledge, pulled himself up, and there before him appeared to be a little old man sitting on a blanket.

"Welcome wayfarer," the old man said, "I have been expecting you."

Wu Li took a deep breath.

"I am Wu Li, best archer in all of China. And… I challenge you!"

The old man, motionless as the mountain itself, smiled, bowed, and looked to the sky.

"Very well, kind sir, as you are my guest, please, go first."

Without hesitation, Wu Li grabbed an arrow from his quiver, notched it on the string of his immense bow, closed his left eye, tilted his head, looked up, drew the string back with all of his might, and let the arrow fly.

As it neared the top of its flight, he pulled a second arrow from the quiver and shot it high overhead, halving the first in two, and, in a rapid succession of ten, continued, each arrow splitting the one before it, arrow halves landing in a perfect circle around the seated Master. Upon entering the ground, the quivering arrow halves made the ancient sound of Om.

"Hmm," said Master Po. "Impressive. Most impressive. Now, I believe, it is my turn."

Reaching behind him (where there would have been a quiver if he had a quiver), he pulled what would have been an arrow (if he had had an arrow), notched what would have been a string on what would have been a bow, closed one eye, pulled slowly back, paused for what seemed like eternity, and then, in slow-motion pantomime, let go.

Smiling ever so slightly, he turned to his challenger.

"You, my friend, have mastered the art of shooting with a bow and arrow. I, on the other hand, have mastered the art of shooting without a bow and arrow."

FOR YOUR REFLECTION:

How much of Wu Li lives inside of you? How much Master Po? And what can you do to become less attached to the fruits of your labor?

I AM *NOT* A HANDYMAN

I am not a handyman. Not even close. And while, indeed, I am a *man* — indeed, considered by many to be a *good* man, I am not even remotely close to being a *handyman*. Yes, I know the difference between a Phillips head screwdriver and a flat head screwdriver. And yes, I have wielded a hammer from time to time without breaking my thumb, but constructing a "bathroom shelving system" has never been my forte, especially a do-it-yourself aluminum bathroom shelving system bought, on sale, in a Mexican hardware store.

It looked so easy when I bought it. But when I opened the box and noticed that the 16-page instruction booklet was, *solamente*, in Spanish, I knew I was in trouble.

Removing the parts from the box, I laid them out on the dining room table and started counting. Excelente! Fantastico! Mucho coolio! Everything was there just as promised! Nothing was missing! And though I must admit I felt like taking a break to celebrate the fact that I had: 1) Successfully opened the box; 2) Placed all of the parts on the dining room table; 3) Counted the parts and; 4) Confirmed the fact that all of the parts that were *supposed* to be in the box actually were in the box, I decided to press on.

It didn't take me long to realize that the 16-page instruction booklet had been written by a dyslexic psychopath with very little appreciation of the fact that I had grown up, Jewish, in the suburbs of New York City. Of the 63 words in Paragraph #1, I recognized only seven. That is approximately 11 percent — excellent, perhaps, for a mutual fund yield, but not so excellent for putting together an aluminum bathroom shelving system before hell freezes over.

"Screw the booklet," I thought to myself. "I don't need no stinking instruction book." I was smart. I was resilient. And I was my own person. And besides, wasn't a picture worth a thousand words? Of course it was! And there, it just so happened, was a picture on every single page! Well, not exactly a picture, but a diagram ... or something sorta kinda *resembling* a *diagram*. Or whatever. Hey, how hard could this be?

So I inserted tube "A" into Tube "B," delayed my celebrational visit to the refrigerator, and inserted Tube "C" into Tube "D."

And while it is absolutely true that the journey of a thousand aluminum tube insertions begins with a single fitting, it soon became apparent that I, newly intoxicated by my recent take-out-all-of-the-parts-from-the-box success, was being *taken in* — not unlike the way inner-city crack dealers give their customers the first taste for free. Clearly, I needed help. And I needed it fast. So I doubled down and returned to the only resource available to me — the 16-page instruction booklet written by the aforementioned nihilistic whack job.

The first line made no sense. Zero. Nada. Zilch. And though I *did* understand the Spanish word for "interior" ("interior"), I did *not* recognize any of the other words. Like "coloque," for instance, no matter how many times I pronounced it. Might it be the south-of-the-border word for "croquet"? Highly doubtful. What about "cologne"? Might coloque have something to do with a Mexican fragrance? Highly doubtful, again. But wait! Hold on! Just three days before, I had downloaded "I Translate" onto my iPhone! All I had to do was type the word and click.

Theoretically, this made perfect sense, or as some of us like to say "senso perfecto," except for the fact that the newly installed Wi-Fi in my house, while it worked just fine on the second and third floors was, shall we say, mucho glitchioso on the *first*.

Not to be deterred, I mounted the stairs, found the signal half way up, and typed in "coloque." Bingo! It meant "place." Whoa! I get it! I'm supposed to *place* something... somewhere... somehow... which although I already knew that, I felt empowered to know it again. Whoo hoo! I was now on my way to having my own *system* for putting together my soon-to-be-installed-in-the-bathroom aluminum shelving system. How cool was that! And the only thing I needed to do was walk half way up the stairs every time I wanted to translate a word which, by my calculations, was going to require about 500 trips — not an especially *efficient* game plan, me being 68 and wanting my aluminum bathroom shelving system installed before Donald Trump built his fucking wall.

That's when it dawned on me. Badabing, badaboom. Like a bolt from the blue. Like Buddha under the Bodhi tree. Like a father understanding that not only will he never get his teenage daughter to clean up her room, *it didn't matter in the least.* I DID NOT HAVE TO DO THIS! I did not have to assemble the do-it-yourself aluminum shelving system on a Thursday afternoon. *Somebody else could do it* — somebody way more qualified than me. Somebody who could actually read Spanish. Somebody who wanted to do it. It didn't have to be me. Nothing was at stake. Nothing at all. Not my manhood. Not my wife's opinion of me. Not even my own opinion of myself. Yes, of course, Jesus, being an enlightened carpenter, could have probably figured it out in a flash — but could he have set up his own Instagram account? Could he have launched his own Facebook group? I doubt it. Hey, sometimes, you just gotta know your limits.

FOR YOUR REFLECTION:

In the Book of Exodus, when Moses asked God what he should say if the people of Israel asked, "What is God's name?" God responded most insightfully, "I am who I am." Wow. Talk about straight shooting!

The modern day correlative of this truth? Oscar Wilde's oft repeated pearl of wisdom: *"Be yourself. Everyone else is taken.*" No matter how hard I have tried to become a handyman or how much I judged myself for not being one, it was never in the cards for me. Just not my thing. And it's absolutely fine that it was not my thing. I also don't play the cello or speak Aramaic. Here's my question to you: *What are you doing that you don't really want to do?* What is your version of not being a handyman? Are you ready to let it go? Anyone you need to declare your new insight to? Oh, one more thing: *Are there any funny stories you want to tell about your repeated efforts to do something you thought you should do, but now that you have read my handyman story, are ready to give up?*

THE FENCE TO NOWHERE

"Good fences make good neighbors," wrote the poet, Robert Frost, 63 years ago, a now iconic poetic meme that looks at both sides of the human condition from two very different perspectives. Yes, it's true, fences make good neighbors. But not always. Sometimes, fences do other things, like make good catalysts to help people understand the distinctions between selfless service, non-attachment, and idiocy.

The year? 1977. The place? Kissimmee, Florida. The occasion? A week-long, outdoor festival of spiritual seekers wanting to experience love. And I was one of them, having traveled 32 hours from Colorado for the chance to listen, learn, and be of service – my chance to "give back" in response to the extraordinary gift I had been given six years earlier by the man all of us had traveled such a long distance to see.

And so, when I arrived, after setting up my tent, I plopped myself down in the "service pool" and waited to be assigned to whatever project needed to be done that day.

I sat there for an hour, doing my best to meditate and stay open to the feeling that whatever was coming my way was going to be perfect. Though relatively new to the so-called spiritual path, I understood that selfless service mattered. And though I had lots of skills to offer, I knew that, somehow, some way, whatever project I would be assigned was going to be the perfect gig for me.

A few minutes later, someone with an air of authority, pointed in my direction, beckoning me forward, and explained that I am part of the fence building crew.

"Hmmm… fence building," I think to myself, "not one of my strengths," my most successful construction project, up to that time, being a letter holder I made for mother in 7th grade.

I walked across the festival grounds to meet the fence building coordinator. The sun was shining. The sky was blue. And I waved at a lot of smiling people. When I arrived, the man in charge – focused, earnest, and glad to see one more able-bodied member of his rapidly forming construction crew – nodded in my direction.

To my left, I noticed a pile of fence posts, a pile that even I could tell was not nearly enough to extend across the massive field.

While my coordinator scurried about, giving each newly arriving volunteer their instructions, I kept staring at the pile of fence posts. True, I was not a carpenter. And true, I had never built a fence across a field, but only an idiot could possibly think there were enough fence posts on that pile to accomplish our goal.

Ah… my first existential question of the day: What to do with my profound insight? What do I say? One option I had, of course, was to say nothing – to simply go with the flow and be a good soldier. Another option was to exit stage right and return to the service pool, hoping to be assigned to a different project with a better chance of success. That's when I remembered a single bit of advice I once heard my teacher say just a few years before – that if I ever saw anyone about to step into a hole and said nothing, it was my fault, not theirs. Bingo! My task now clear – all I had to do was approach the earnest, fence-building coordinator and inform him, that based on my calculations, we were all about to step into a very big hole – that, simply put, there weren't enough fence posts to build a fence across the field. Case closed.

My input, to say the least, was not well-received. With a blank expression on his face, the earnest, young, fence-building coordinator handed me a post-hole digger and told me what to do.

I paused. The moment of truth was upon me. Do I begin working on a project I knew, from the outset, was doomed? Or do I just let go, trust the process, and see what happens? Besides, I thought to myself, there was always a chance that I didn't have all the information I needed to make a wise decision. Maybe a new supply of fence posts would be delivered later that day.

Or maybe another crew of fence builders, from the opposite side of the field, was going to meet us half way. Or maybe, just maybe, my fence post calculations were seriously flawed.

And so I began.

It felt good digging holes in the ground. Good to sweat. Good to serve. Good to let go of the self-talk in my head. But even as I grunted and groaned, in the back of my mind, I knew that the reason why all of us were being employed in the first place was highly questionable.

The project continued for three days. From morning to night. In good weather and bad. Six of us dug. Six of us carried. Six of us stuck fence posts in the ground. No new fence posts arrived. No extra crew of fence builders magically appeared to meet us half way. The field did not get any smaller.

On the third day, when we ran out of materials, the six of us, dirty, sweaty, and exhausted, stepped back and stared at the fence. As I predicted, it extended only halfway across the field, a kind of Andy Goldsworthy installation, a bit of performance art that would have made a Zen master laugh.

Two hours later, when the festival officially began, I witnessed hundreds of people, approaching from a distance. The "fence" we built had absolutely no effect on them. They noticed what seemed to be a fence, but since it only extended halfway across the field, they simply walked around it. It kept no one out and no one in.

For Your Reflection:

What big effort have you made in your life that did not exactly turn out the way you thought it was supposed to? *And what, if anything, have you learned from that experience?*

ALMOST DROWNING

The average life span of a white American male is 76.7, the same age T.S. Eliot was when he died and Albert Einstein and Ruben Hurricane Carter. Forty-nine years ago, I almost screwed up that average. I wasn't planning on dying that day. Really, I wasn't. The only thing I was planning on was picking up my girlfriend, Connie, and driving to the most secluded beach I could find. She was 19. I was 21. And we had the rest of our lives to look forward to, or so we thought.

The ride to the beach was straight out of a coming of age movie. The top was down. The music was loud. And her left hand was resting on my right thigh. If there had been a movie director in the back seat, he'd have been standing up, yelling "wrap," and fantasizing about the sequel. But there was no director in the back seat, only a cooler and a blanket, which I soon found myself carrying as Connie and I made our way through the summer woods to a beach only the locals knew about. Ten minutes later, we were running headlong into the ocean, screaming at the top of our lungs, buoyed by the waves, the sea spray, and the vast expanse of sky overhead.

I have no idea how long this went on. All I know is when I finally looked at Connie, then 20 yards away from me, I saw panic in her eyes.

"Cramp!" I thought to myself. "She's got a cramp." I put my head down and swam as fast as I could towards her. When I got there, all she could do was stare at me. She could not speak. Not a word. I had no idea what was wrong, but knew something needed to happen fast, so I made my way behind her, cupped my hand over her chin like I had seen on TV, and started swimming, one-armed, to the shore.

I went nowhere. The only movement I was making was in my mind – the sudden realization that I needed to make a choice. Do I play the hero and try to save her or do I go for help?

Neither of us spoke She looked at me and I looked at her. And then, without a word, I turned and stared swimming towards the shore.

I wanted to get there as fast as I could, but swimming straight ahead was no longer an option. Undertow! Diagonal was the only way to go. So I lifted one arm and then the next, gulping air faster and faster, feeling only the weight of the world.

And then, with almost no strength left, I saw, rising from the sea, like some kind of mirage, a gigantic rock, a sudden island of reprieve no more than 30 yards away. The shore was no longer my destination. Now it was rock. Just the rock. If... only I... could... get to... the rock... I could... catch my breath and rest. That's when an unseen wave lifted my body up and slammed it down on the rock, me now spread-eagled like a madman, hugging the stone, gasping, and holding on for dear life. All I wanted was a breath. Just one more breath. That was it. That was all I wanted. Just one more breath and a brief chance to rest.

A thousand pinpricks penetrated my flesh, then green sea moss beneath me. There was nothing to hold onto, nothing for my fingers to grab. And then the next wave came and washed me off that rock into the ocean once again. My body? Vertical now. No longer swimming, I was *climbing*, like a man on fire, an invisible ladder in space. I grabbed for rungs, clutching for something, anything, to hold onto. But there was nothing to hold. No ladder. No rungs. No hand. My mouth opened, but only water rushed in. I grabbed at the air once again, trying to climb, trying to breathe, but only water enters me and... I... am... going down. *I don't want to die! I don't! I don't want to die!* I flail and scramble to the surface, gasping for one more breath. And then? EVERYTHING STOPS. EVERYTHING COMPLETELY STOPS. I look at the shore and a single thought rushes through my mind. *"You will die here and people will remember you as the person who died here."* That was it, my final epitaph, a cautionary tale parents would tell their children every time they passed this God forsaken beach. I kept looking and looking at the shore and then, I completely understood.

My life has been nothing more than a cartoon. Nothing has been real – until now! And I'm just about to die.

Every cell in my body is awake, every synapse firing. Every fiber of my being has snapped to attention and begs for one more breath. The joke is on me! For the first time in my life I am completely alive and I am just about to die. And then…. rising from who knows where, something I have no words for and never will, some kind of primal power from the great beyond takes me over completely. It closes my eyes. It moves my arms. It breathes the air, me a puppet at the end of its very long string, with only one quest: "GET TO THE SHORE! GET TO THE SHORE!"

The next thing I know I'm swimming in water only knee deep, the child's end of the pool. I stand and stumble to the beach, looking for help. But no one is there. No one. There is not a single soul, only an infinite expanse of emptiness and space. And then… the only word that remained in my vocabulary came flying out of my mouth: "HELP!" it screamed, "HELP!!! HELP!!!!

To my right, maybe 30 yards away, a young woman slowly moved in my direction. She seems slightly stoned. Now, we're face to face. "HELP!!!!" I scream again, trying to explain with the only word left in my world. HELLPPP!!!! *It is not working.* She does not understand what I am trying to say. So I turn around and point at the horizon. But… there… is… no one… there. No one is there! No one. Only waves and foam and a few seagulls gliding overhead. That's when I died for the first time. Yes, my body was standing, but my soul was gone. How can this be happening to me? How can I still be alive, but not Connie? HOW? And then... praise the Lord and the Mother of God, far off in the distance, we see her head bobbing in the waves, just above the water line. She's alive! She's alive! Connie is alive!

The woman standing beside me and her boyfriend, who has somehow appeared, run as fast as they can into the ocean and pull Connie out. They carry her to our blanket and lay her gently down. They stay a minute, ask us how we are, and continue on their way.

Now it's just Connie and me. The first thing we did was kneel and kiss the ground. Then we start singing children's songs – every song we know. For an hour, that's all we did. Sing! SING! "Jingle Bells." "Happy Birthday to You." "Row, Row, Row Your Boat." Whatever we knew. Sing! That's all we did. Sing! Then Connie started throwing up. Then we just lay there, in silence, next to each other, under the sun and the cloudless blue sky. That's it. We just lay there, stunned to be breathing the air we no longer needed to gulp.

FOR YOUR REFLECTION:

As I was going down for the third time, the only thing I wanted was one more breath, one more chance to be alive. Everything else I had come to call my life had completely disappeared – every thought, every fear, every hope, desire, dream, regret, and aspiration was gone. The only thing that remained was the primal and very naked will to live. What it was that saved me, I do not know. Some people call it God.

Some call it destiny, karma, or Grace. I don't know what to call it and, the older I get, the less important it is that I give a name to what it was my mind will never comprehend. All I know is this: deep within me and deep within you and deep within each and every one of us on this beautiful blue planet is an untapped reservoir of strength, a fifth gear, a hidden chamber of the soul.

Rarely do we go there. The need does not arise. And so, we rely on what we already know, which, for most of us, gets us through life. But "getting through life" is not the reason we are here. Life is not something to get through. Life is a chance to become completely alive, a chance to wake up from our trance and actually LIVE, to truly experience the unnamable power that gives us life and has the kindness to save us from whatever it is we find ourselves drowning in – be it the ocean, hopelessness, fear, despair, anger, sadness, a broken marriage, debt, a dead-end job, or the toxic state of the world these days. Who at some point in their life doesn't find themselves drowning? Who? Drowning is not the issue, my friends. The issue is what do we do when we find ourselves going under? Do we go down for the third time or do we tap into that hidden source of strength that brings us to the shore? And then, when we get there, do we stand on our own two feet and CALL FOR HELP, even when it seems like there is no one there to hear our pleas?

In *your* life, what have you been drowning in? How does it feel – REALLY feel? And what can you do today to ask for the help you need? And for those of you, like me, who have almost literally drowned, what was that experience like? What did you *feel* going down? How were you saved? What did you learn? *And how is what you learned still serving you today or could serve you today if you allowed yourself to fully remember the moment you were taking your last breath?*

BARNEY AND THE GATEKEEPERS

My father, a pharmacist by profession, retired to Florida at the age of 55. His retirement lasted three weeks. After a lifetime's worth of waking up each morning with a purpose, now he had none. Golf didn't count. Nor did watering his lawn or reading *People Magazine*. In fact, nothing counted. Without having something to do that had meaning for him, my father was very much lost at sea. And so, he decided, one fine air-conditioned day, to begin importing exotic foreign cars. The business model was a simple one. Buy low. Sell high.

As his only son, I was impressed. Mercedes were not only way cooler than nose drops, there was a much bigger profit margin. Plus, who knows, it was always possible that one of them might trickle down to me one day.

My dad's foreign car venture lasted six months.

Now 56 and, again, unemployed, he decided to take a left turn and open an art gallery with my mother, a move that shocked the entire family. It wasn't fine art they were selling, mind you. It was *decorative* art – the kind that newly retired people were in search of to match their living room couch. Like maybe something in green.

That venture lasted two years.

Now, closing in on 60, with two false starts under his belt and a shrinking nest egg, my father decided it was time to get his real estate license. After all, he reasoned, the building boom was huge in Florida and somebody had to sell all those houses, right, so why not him?

Getting his real estate license was easy. He studied. He took the test. He passed. Getting customers? Not so easy.

With tons of other real estate agents to compete with, he needed a creative way to differentiate himself from the competition. Newspaper ads were out. Too expensive. TV commercials were out. Also, too expensive. And so, in honor of Willie Sutton, the bank robber who once replied "That's where the money is" when asked why he robbed banks, my dad launched his West Palm Beach *gatekeeper campaign*.

Here's how it worked: Armed with nothing but his electric yellow business cards, he made the rounds to the guardhouses of the most popular gated communities in the area. After the requisite amount of schmoozing, he introduced himself as "Barney the Real Estate Agent," handed a stack of cards to each gatekeeper and declared, "If you ever meet anyone looking to buy a house, give them my card. For each person you refer who buys a house from me, I will give you $100."

Once a month, after that, my father would make the rounds again, bringing each security guard a fresh supply of business cards and a hot pizza. Soon, he had a "sales force" of 25 armed security guards representing him, a uniformed crew of highly knowledgeable locals perfectly positioned to introduce him to hundreds of the house-buying public.

Two years later, my father was making more money as a retiree than he ever made during his prime. He worked until he was 89.

FOR YOUR REFLECTION:

I am now the age my father was 15 years into his retirement. Like him, I find great meaning in work. Like him, I have gone through my own rites of passage. And like him, I cannot afford to hire a sales force to get the word out about the services I provide. Which is why I have, in honor of the man who brought me into the world, just launched my own version of my father's gatekeeper campaign. Maybe it will work and maybe it won't, but I just love the feeling of reprising his idea and tweaking it for the times.

This is just one more reason why stories are such powerful agents of communication. First, the story I have just told expresses how I remember my father's experience. Secondly, the story helps me reflect on its meaning and apply it to my own life. And third, by telling the story, I have shared its wisdom with you. Who knows? Maybe my father's experience, 40 years ago, communicated to you as a story will be enough to get your own wheels turning while you figure out a newer, cooler, simpler way to get the word out about the service you provide.

What "unusual suspects" in your life, might make for good referral agents – people who can help you get the word out about what you do and, somehow, be compensated for their efforts?

MY SISTER, PREM RAWAT, AND ME

I first heard about Prem Rawat when I was 23 and he was 13. At that time, he was known as "Maharaji" and I was known as "Ditty." Though he was barely a teen, I found him to be extraordinarily wise, well beyond his years. Actually, I found him to be more than wise, because he wasn't just talking about the eternal verities of life, he sparked a palpable experience of peace, love, and joy.

And so, at 24, I decided to follow up on his offer and "receive Knowledge" – his phrase for inner awakening. It was, for me, beyond all doubt, the most extraordinary day of my life.

Newly supercharged and supremely confident that I had just discovered the secret of life, I called my sister to explain why it would be a good idea for her to follow in my steps. It went over like a lead balloon. Make that two lead balloons. Though both of us had grown up in the same house, our bedrooms next to each other, we were now, apparently, living on different planets, her perception of me alternating between well-meaning flake, long-haired hippie, and baby boomer going through yet another phase.

Fifteen years passed.

She had three children. I had none. She lived in the suburbs. I lived in the woods. She watched TV. I watched the moon. Finding it painful for my grand declarations about the path I was on to fall on deaf ears, I stopped talking about Prem Rawat in my sister's presence. But then, in 1988, upon hearing that he was going to be speaking at Lincoln Center in New York City, just 20 miles from where she lived, I couldn't resist and invited her to join me.

"What the hell?" I thought to myself. "The worst thing that could happen is she says NO." But she didn't say no. She said YES and agreed to meet me in the lobby of Avery Fisher Hall on the appointed day just a few weeks away. I was thrilled.

Settling into our seats as the hall filled up, my sister and I made some small talk, agreeing, once again, just how crazy our parents were. And then the lights dimmed, Prem walked out on stage, sat on his chair, adjusted his mic, and began. Though I'd heard him speak at least 100 times before, he seemed to be in rare form that night, starting with a joke or two, a light-hearted story, and some funny remarks about *New Yawk*. The audience loved it. And so did my sister. Three minutes into his talk, she turned to me and spoke eight words I will never forget for as long as I live. "You never told me how funny he was."

This was my sister's first real introduction to Prem Rawat. *This* was her initiation, laughing her tushie off in the third row of Avery Fisher Hall. Somehow, the man she had once assumed would be impossible to understand had *gotten her to laugh.* And laugh she did. Not titters, not chuckles or guffaws, but out and out, from the core of her being, laughter. I just sat there, stunned at how, in just a few minutes, the man she thought was only for her whacky younger brother had sparked a wonderful opening in her.

Over the next 20 years, Phyllis accompanied me to five more Prem Rawat events. After the fifth, she asked me if there were any videos of him speaking that she could watch. I sent her the links. She watched them and told me, now and again, how much she enjoyed what he had to say. A year later, she asked if there was any way she could receive Knowledge. I sent her the info and six months later she did just that.

When she passed away a few years later, I sat by her bed for eight days straight, a small picture of Prem Rawat on her bedside table. I rubbed her feet. We cried. We laughed. And when it was time to go, she did. Peacefully.

FOR YOUR REFLECTION:

Some things take a while. The proverbial river we try so hard to push is actually better suited for swimming. Whatever it is that you have experienced in this life is wonderful. Treasure it. But it's *your* experience, not someone else's. Relax. Let go. Let it flow. What will be will be.

FRENCH CAMEMBERT

As the story goes, Camembert was originally created in 1791 by Marie Harel, a dairy farmer from Normandy upon receiving some advice from a priest from Brie. Its unique smell has been variably described as funky, mushroom-like, earthy, foul, stinky, and the secret project of a chemical company. Camembert is made from unpasteurized milk and is rich in chemicals like ammonia, sodium chloride, and succinic acid. It is rated, by a leading food blog, as the second stinkiest cheese in the world, just behind Pont l'Evesque. Even when it's wrapped in its fashionable French box and the box stashed in an unfashionable plastic container in the frig, it still smells to high heaven.

If you've never tried it, here's all you need to know: Camembert is to American cheese as Lady Gaga is to Marie Osmond. In France, Camembert has become something of a cult. It isn't just consumed, it's worshipped, talked about, I would venture to say, more than Jesus. That is, if the past two weeks of staying with my French relatives is any indication. In America, where I come from, cheese is something to slap on a hamburger or serve to guests before dinner so they don't get cranky. In France, cheese is eaten *after* the meal. It's a *course*, not a snack – an orgasm, not a peck on the cheek. Fine. All well and good. In the cheese world, Camembert is royalty. OK. I get it. But, as a visiting New Yorker, what I find most astounding about Camembert is its capacity to bridge the intergenerational gap. Put three generations of French people around the dinner table – all with very different tastes in music, fashion, technology, TV shows, and politics – and, with the presence of Camembert, you will soon experience something akin to the beginning of world peace. As they all inhale the scent of Camembert and the soft, round, glowing, buttery, wheel of cheese begins its magic, all other conversations cease.

Where just minutes before people were arguing about the economy, the weather, or terrorism, a kind of familial harmonic resonance occurs when the Camembert appears. All eyes are on the cheese. All comments are about the cheese. The Camembert becomes the sun around which the rest of us revolve. The aches and pains of my 90-year-old mother-in-law? The late night debates about how to find her a live-in companion or what it will take to convince her to move into an assisted living facility? Gone. All gone. Dissolved. Disappeared. Only cheese exists, *or*, to be more specific, *Camembert*.

FOR YOUR REFLECTION:

Think about your family for a moment. What is their Camembert – the one commonly agreed upon, shared reference point that dissolves all differences? *How can you introduce more of this into your visit the next time your family gets together?*

THE INFINITE GLASS OF WATER

Once upon a time there was a young disciple of a great Master who found himself wrestling with a very difficult question, one that would not go away no matter how much he contemplated it. Though he had asked all the senior monks in the monastery that had been his home for the past 20 years, no one had an answer, which rang true for him. And so, one fine spring day, gathering up all of his courage, he decided to approach the Master himself.

"Oh Illustrious One," the monk began, "for years I have been listening to your discourses. Time and again, you have referred to something called *Maya*, the great illusion we are supposedly all bound by, but still I do not understand. Please, sir, can you explain to me what is this Maya of which you speak?"

"Oh, my son," the Master replied, "yours is an excellent question. Most penetrating and timely, too. Yes, I will be happy to provide an answer. But before I do, I have one simple request. Can you bring me a glass of water? I am very thirsty."

The young monk smiled, nodded his head, and, with a simple bow, exited to secure the glass of water.

His first instinct was an obvious one – to walk to the well in the center of the monastery courtyard and draw the water. Upon reflection, however, he soon realized there was another, better source of water, just a little further up the road in a neighboring village.

"If I am going to get water for my Master," the young monk reasoned, "it has got to be the best."

And so, with a one-pointedness of focus he had never felt as deeply before, he began his journey.

The neighboring village, known not only for the purity of its water, but also for its breathtaking views, was not far, but the road to it, washed out by a recent storm, was difficult to traverse and so the journey took just a little longer than he had expected. Fortunately, when the monk arrived, just a few minutes before sundown, there were only three people on line at the well.

Thankful for his good fortune, he closed his eyes and turned his attention within, hearing only the sound of his breathing and then, from who knows where, the sound of sobbing.

Surprised, he opened his eyes and noticed a crying young woman, standing in line before him.

"Dear lady," the monk offered, leaning closer, "what seems to be the problem?"

"It is my father," she replied. "He is very ill and nothing I do seems to help. I am besides myself with grief."

The monk nodded. "Yes, I understand. The body ages and declines. It is always sad to see our loved ones suffering, especially those who have brought us into this world."

For a moment, the two of them just stood there in silence, both at a loss for what to say. Then the woman spoke.

"Kind sir," she began, "I see, by your robes, that you are a monk. Is it true, as I've heard, that those of your order are masters of the healing arts?"

"Yes, it is true, dear woman. From an early age, we are taught many things: how to chant, how to pray, how to meditate, how to read the stars, and how to heal with herbs and balms, both of which I carry wherever I go."

The eyes of the young woman opened wider as she stepped forward and touched the monk lightly on the arm. "If it is agreeable to you, kind sir, would you, after drawing your water, accompany me ever so briefly to my father's house? Perhaps your healing touch is all he needs to stay alive."

Having been taught, for years, the power of service and compassion, the young monk's path was clear. "Of course!" he replied. "How could I refuse such a heartfelt request? Please, dear lady, lead the way."

It was only a short walk to her father's house, a small, well-kept cottage on the outskirts of town. One look at the old man was all it took for the monk to see the seriousness of the situation. Clearly, the man was at death's door and, unless the monk began immediately tending to his needs, it was obvious that the young woman would be fatherless by morning.

And so, all night the monk sat by the old man's bedside, administering herbs and teas and balms, rubbing his feet, chanting sacred mantras, and, all the while, abiding in a state of deep meditation.

At daybreak, when the young woman woke, she was amazed to see her father smiling, talking with the monk, the color of life having returned to his face. Bowing deeply, she embraced her father, stroked his hair, and kissed him lightly on the cheek.

"Praise God!" she cried. "And praise you, oh holy monk!"

"Thank you, dear woman. I appreciate your kind words, but it is not me that heals. It is the power of life and your father's will to live. But please know this: Your father is not yet healed. Last night was just a beginning. By my calculations, he will need at least three more days of care before he is back on his feet."

Three days. That was the monk's prediction. Not a long time to return from death's door. But on the fourth day, much to the monk's surprise, the father took a turn for the worse and died.

THE INFINITE GLASS OF WATER

But grief was only part of what consumed her. Fear also had its way with her. You see, with her father gone, there would be no one to run his shop of fine textiles in the center of town and with no one to run his shop, there would be no money to buy food and firewood, and with no food and firewood, the young woman would not only starve to death, but freeze, with winter fast approaching.

"Oh monk, sent to us from God," she exclaimed on the fourth day after her father's passing, "I know what I am about to say is a lot to ask, but would you be willing to mind my father's shop for the next few days so I can get my house in order? The task is really quite a simple one. All you need to do is greet the people who enter the shop, help them find what they want, and sell it to them at a mutually agreeable price. In the meantime, I will fix you a bed in the barn so you will have a comfortable place to rest and meditate upon your return each night."

"I accept your kind invitation, dear woman. Remember, I have been trained to serve ever since I was a small boy. It's off to work I go. May God be with you on this glorious day."

One day turned to two. Two turned to four. And four turned to eight. Not only did the business grow with the young monk's loving care, so did his feelings for the woman. In time, his appreciation turned to fondness, his fondness turned to attraction, and his attraction turned to love. A year later they married and a few years after that they found themselves the proud parents of two beautiful children, a boy and a girl, both of whom the town elders claimed to be incarnations of great spiritual beings.

The young monk, now merchant and father, could not remember a time in his life when he had ever felt so happy.

Five years passed. Then another ten. In the 16th year of his adventure into love, 80 miles from his home on yet another buying mission, a sudden summer storm came upon the land. Not just any storm, but a storm the ferocity of which had never been seen before. It rained for days.

At first, the merchant simply buttoned up his coat, opened an umbrella, and trudged on, committed as he was to bringing home the finest of the region's textiles to his ever-growing store, especially since he had already taken advance orders from some of the town's most influential citizens. But no matter how steadfast he continued to be, the river continued to rise. And as it did, the keen-eyed merchant noticed three large bags of rice floating by him, bags marked with the insignia of his well-respected enterprise.

"This is not good," he said to himself. "Not good at all. It seems the river has breached one of my silos. I must turn for home."

The rain kept coming. The river kept rising. And, as it did, he noticed it carried more than bags of rice downstream. It also carried cows, three of which he recognized as his own.

"Not good, not good at all," he exclaimed again, digging his heels deeper into the side of his trusty steed and quickening his pace once again.

And then, yet another mile closer to home, he saw a sight he couldn't have imagined in a thousand years. There in the river, face up and unmoving, floated his young daughter and son.

"Oh my God," he wailed. "How can this be? My two precious children, gone. GONE!"

The man had never felt such grief before, never such loss – his only motivation to gallop as fast as he could and return to the love of his life, the one who would be waiting for him, arms wide open, at home, his sweet and precious wife.

Yes, he saw her, but sooner than expected. There, not more than a few yards from where he now stood, he saw her floating down the river, face up, unmoving, body bloated from a watery death.

Devastated beyond belief, he did what any man in his situation would have done and threw himself headlong into the river. He saw no reason to live anymore. Nor did he see, upon throwing himself into the water, a large piece of timber floating by. The impact of his head hitting this unseen piece of wood was strong enough to knock him out, the large piece of timber now a kind of makeshift raft carrying him downstream.

How long he floated no one knows for sure. Nor does anyone know where that miraculous piece of wood came to rest on the far riverbank. But come to rest it did. Was he dead or alive? He could not tell. Shivering and stunned, all he could see when he opened his eyes was wet sand and what appeared to be a pair of feet. Rubbing his eyes, he continued staring at the feet now strangely familiar to him. Raising his head ever so slightly, he saw ankles, then the hem of a robe, and then, looking up all the way, the radiant face of a man looking down at him and smiling.

"Do you have my glass of water?" the man asked. "My son, many years ago you asked me to help you understand the meaning of Maya. What you have experienced these past 18 years has been just one second of it. Welcome home!"

FOR YOUR REFLECTION:

Looking back at your life, what might you have forgotten about your original mission or purpose? In what ways might you have gotten distracted along the way? *And what, if anything, can you do, these days, to fetch that glass of water?*

ROBBERS

When I was 13, my sister was 18, the proverbial big sister. I was the proverbial little brother. And though she called me "twerp" and I called her "fatso," it was always comforting to know she was in the next room, especially on the nights when our parents went out. I wouldn't be alone. My sister was there.

But when she went off to college, everything changed. Now I was the only child in the house. Now it was just me.

I will never forget my first night alone. My parents, after dinner, casually informed me that they were going out for the evening, but would be back at a reasonable hour. They petted the dog, gave me a hug, and were gone in a flash. I stood by the front door, listening, until the sound of their Oldsmobile disappeared into the distance. Then I made myself a huge bowl of ice cream, retreated to my room, turned on the TV, flopped down on my bed, and started doing my homework.

So far so good. The ice cream was yummy. The capital of Montana was Helena, and the Mets were leading 4-2. That's when I started hearing the sounds, very strange sounds coming from the kitchen – troubling sounds, scary sounds, the kind robbers make when looking for things to steal. Like my mother's set of sterling silver, for example, the extremely expensive set of sterling silver given to her years ago by my rich Uncle Herman.

The sounds from the kitchen continued, sounds I had never heard before. And then... absolutely nothing... nothing at all... just silence... a deadly silence... the kind that could only mean one thing: the robbers had just poisoned my dog. Or strangled her.

Now the moment of truth was upon me. Laying on my bed, eating the last of my ice cream, I had a decision to make. A big one. Do I turn up the sound of my TV so the robbers would know that someone was home and leave on their own, or do I confront them, saving my mother's sterling silver before they get away?

It may have seemed like a choice, but it wasn't. I knew, in my heart of hearts, there was only one thing to do. So I got off my bed and began making my way, ninja-like, oh so slowly, out of my room, down the hallway, past the bathroom, closer and closer to the closed kitchen door. My heart was pounding, my breath coming faster, my mind racing. Standing just a foot from the door, I stopped and listened. An eternity passed. The sounds from the kitchen continued. And then, raising my right leg, I kicked open the door and leaped into the kitchen, letting out the kind of scream karate masters make when they attack.

The first thing I saw was my dog, looking up at me, wagging her tail. She was alive! Alive! I bent down to pet her, no robbers in sight, having obviously heard me coming and vamoosed out the side door. I stood up and walked a few steps to the table where the sterling silver set was supposed to be in its velvety blue box. It was there, just a few inches away from the spice rack and the stack of *Life Magazines*. I opened it slowly. Not a fork or spoon was missing. Not a knife. I made my way to the pantry and gave my dog a treat. Then I returned to my room, finished my ice cream, memorized the capital of Vermont (Montpelier) and watched the end of the baseball game. Then I turned on my clock radio and went to bed.

This same drama must have played itself out at least 40 times in the next two years. My strategy, I must say, worked like a charm. From the time I was 13 until I was 15, when I stopped playing this little game, not a single thing was ever stolen from our house.

For Your Reflection:

This story of mine happened 57 years ago. For the six decades that followed, only two people ever heard about it – my best friend, Matt and my wife, Evelyne. And yet, for me, now 70, taking the time to reflect on this story and share it with you has been a revelation. While laughable in many ways, I've gotten some keen insights into my own psyche and how I, at an early age, became wired to deal with the unknown, whether real or imagined. My self-invented rite-of-passage was how I learned to deal with fear and the choices before me. First, I learned I needed to be alert to the clues all around me. Then I learned I had a choice. Then I learned I had to choose. Once my choice was made, everything was cool. I was no longer a victim, no longer a boy hiding in his room, but a man of action. And the danger? Gone.

What, in your life, these days, is sparking fear? And how successful are your efforts in addressing it?

ONE PERSON AT A TIME

My teacher, Prem Rawat, is a marvelous storyteller. From what I can gather, he tells three kinds of stories: 1) jokes, which are the shortest kind of stories; 2) classic teaching tales that have been told for centuries, and; 3) his own, personal accounts of meaningful moments in his life. All three of these types of story pack a wallop. All three, delivered at the right time in the right way, have the potential to uplift, awaken, and inspire.

The following story, which I heard Prem tell years ago, has stayed with me from the moment I heard it. I continue to drink from the fountain of this story, refreshed and renewed every time I do. It's a story about his father, Shri Hans Ji Maharaj, a great Teacher of his time in India, and a few of his students.

In the 1960s, a handful of Shri Hans's students, thrilled at the prospect that he would be visiting their village in a few months, made an extraordinary effort to "get the word out" to a massive amount of people in the region. They handed out flyers, nailed posters to trees, organized introductory events, and did whatever else it took to alert as many people as possible. These were very exciting times for these devotees, moved as they were by the all-too-rare opportunity to pave the way for their Teacher's imminent arrival.

Months passed. They worked around the clock, focused on just one thing – inviting as many people as possible to listen to their Master's discourse. Then the big day came, the day they had been so diligently planning for. Everything was together – the tickets, the ushers, the seating, the food, and the music. Everything. But much to their surprise, only *one* person showed up. Just one. Just one person. Totally disappointed, guilty, and experiencing who knows how many other painful emotions, they approached their Teacher, solemnly, to deliver the bad news.

Shri Maharaji just sat there, listening. Then he smiled broadly.

"OK," he said, "Very well. But do you know *how long* this one person has waited to hear my message?"

FOR YOUR REFLECTION:

One person. That was it. Only one person showed up after months of extraordinary effort. But the Master was not disappointed. Neither was he sad, upset, or judging anyone for the apparent lack of results. One person was sufficient for him. One. His was not a numbers game. His was something else. He was not measuring success the way most of us do. He was coming from an entirely different mindset – one that was filled with love, presence, and gratitude for the opportunity to share his message, even if there was only one person in the audience.

Maybe one day I will understand this. And maybe one day I will actually live this expression of truth. My strategy, historically, has been different. I conceive great goals. I make long lists. I execute a bunch of tasks in service to my great goals and, more often than not, there is a gap between my goals and what actually happens. Committed to a particular outcome, I usually end up feeling, much like Shri Hans's students years ago, *disappointed* – like I could have done better, way better. Like I blew it.

The older I get, the more I realize how flawed this way of thinking is. Having audacious goals is fine. There's nothing wrong with having big goals. But it's the *attachment* to these goals where things start getting strange.

While it's been years since I've heard Prem Rawat tell this story, I cannot get it out of my mind. And I don't want to. It's a lesson I need to keep on learning – going beyond the numbers and entering into the place where gratitude reigns – the place where even one person showing up, or none, is not only sufficient, but divine.

THE BOOK I WANTED TO BUY MY MOTHER

For many years I wanted to buy a book for my mother, a book that would explain *everything* – what I hadn't or couldn't explain since I had been old enough to notice my mother wasn't all that happy and, Lord knows, I wanted my mother to be happy, and, if not "happy" per se, then at least aware of what it was that made me, her son, happy, the thing that, for so many years, she thought was just a phase I was going through, and, even worse, some kind of heartless rejection of her and her way of life.

Yes, I wanted to buy my mother a book that would explain it all, the whole "New Age thing," the whole "Guru thing," the whole   "It's-OK-I-don't-eat-your-veal-parmigiana-anymore-because-I'm-a-vegetarian" thing.

Somebody must have written it. Somebody must have noticed the market niche of mothers who worry why their high performing sons have gone spiritual.

And so, I went looking for the book. Like some people look for God.

And though I never found it, I did find some reasonable facsimiles – cleverly titled books displayed by the check-out counter, conceived by marketing geniuses who somehow knew my need, the need a son has to make his mother smile, the book that would keep his mother company during those long, cold nights when her husband was working late and her children were asleep and there was nothing good on TV – the ultimate self-help book that would remove her worries, her doubts, and her exponentially growing fears of thinking her son had not only gone off the deep end but would never come back.

I wanted my mother to know how beautiful life was and how simple it could be to experience that beauty. I wanted her to know there was something timeless within her, something beyond the stress of aging, beyond early bird dinners and the too-careful clipping of newspaper coupons.

Maybe it was selfish of me, but I wanted to buy my mother a book that would deliver some proof that love was the name of the game and that (bite your tongue and spit three times) the act of "turning within" was as good for you as chicken soup.

During my stay with my father after my mother's funeral, I discovered, in oh-so-many places around their house, the books I had given her for the past 35 years. Most of them had never been opened. Like some strange mix of faded Stonehenge rubble, they lay in piles everywhere – on her night table, on her desk, stuffed behind cookbooks, in the garage. Some, when you opened them, still had that new book crackling sound.

I felt sad that she hadn't read them, sad, and the kind of low-grade resignation teenagers feel when they realize their parents just don't get it.

FOR YOUR REFLECTION:

Now, some 15 years later, older and just a bit wiser, I realize that no book would have ever been enough to give my mother. It wasn't the books she didn't read. It was the act of *giving* them to her and what the giving represented. I wanted my mother to have the *experience* the books were describing. As my long-time teacher is fond of saying, "if you are thirsty, it's water that you need, not the description of water." And ultimately, isn't that what it's all about, helping the people we love find the water? *What is it that you really want to give your loved ones?*

ETERNITY AND THE TOLEDO ON-RAMP

The spiritual literature of Planet Earth is full of stories that track the trials and tribulations of earnest souls on the path to God. Like Jonah in the belly of the whale. Like Moses in the desert. Like Jesus on the cross. Every culture has their own, just like they have their own creation myths and favorite cheese. Indeed, the heroes and heroines of these soul-shaping stories have, in time, become a kind of code for the hard-to-describe qualities that define what it means to be an evolving human being – the kind of stories we tell our kids whenever we want to impress on them something timeless and profound.

Good. We need stories. We need memorable examples of what's possible. What we don't need, however, is the assumption that only stories in the scriptures are stories worth telling. They're not the only ones. Each of us, in our own curious way, has had similar experiences – modern-day versions of the archetypal challenges that try the souls of all men and women. Like the time, as a hitchhiker, I stood on the on ramp to I-70, in Toledo, Ohio, for ten hours, without a ride – just the hot sun overhead and the creeping sense that God, if there was a God, didn't really like me all that much.

What I didn't understand at the time was that there was a divine choreography at play, one that transcended my pinhole view of life.

The day started off quite innocently enough, in Montreal, Canada, 1,729 miles from where I lived, listening to a very inspiring man speak to 3,000 people about the origins of peace. It was a good day, a very good day, a day that filled me with joy and gratitude. After a good night's sleep in a modestly priced hotel, I began the long journey home, hitchhiking back to Colorado, with my friend, Danny.

In only three minutes we got our first ride. We simply stuck out our thumbs and stopped a green Toyota, a pleasant young salesman behind the wheel. He shook our hands. He talked about his work. He gave us each a tuna on rye. Badaboom. Badabing. There was a God! Five hundred and sixty nine miles later, just outside of Toledo, our paths parted and our first ride of the day bid us adieu.

The on-ramp to the interstate, which is where he dropped us off, was rather unexceptional. No movie was going to be made there that day, no marriage proposals. Just two young, God-intoxicated men with their thumbs out, trying to get back to Denver before their money ran out.

One hour passed. Then another. Then another after that. Not a single car stopped or even slowed down. Many other hitchhikers came and went. But not us. We just stood there. If this was a junior high school dance, we were the fat girls with braces.

"Yo, Danny," I blurted, you know what this reminds me of?"

"No, what?" Danny said.

"*Siddhartha.*"

"Herman Hesse's *Siddartha*?" he responded.

"Yes! Herman Hesse's *Siddhartha.*"

"Really?" Danny replied. "And why is that?"

"Because," I said, "Siddhartha once said there were three things he had learned in life that had saved his butt. First, he could *fast*. Second, he could *wait*. And, third, he could *meditate*. So today, my good friend, we get to practice one third of Siddhartha's yoga – waiting. How cool is that?"

Another hour passed. Then another. Then another after that. If you are counting, dear reader, we are now in our sixth hour without a ride on the Toledo on-ramp.

One thing was becoming clear: Whatever Danny and I were doing wasn't working. So we decided it was time to experiment. First, Danny stood and I sat. Then I stood and Danny sat. Then we made a sign with "Denver or Bust" on it. Then we pretended to pray. Then Danny hoisted me on his shoulders. Then I hoisted him on mine. Nothing worked. If this had been a coming-of-age movie, all of this would have been quite funny, especially the way the director would have sped up the film to give a kind of Charlie Chaplin-esque quality to it. But this was not a coming-of-age movie. There was no director, no film crew, no catering tent. There was only the two of us, the mid-afternoon sun shimmering off of the burning concrete, making everything look like a mirage.

While Danny continued fixing his gaze on the oncoming cars, I found myself looking up at the sky and talking to myself. Was I being punished? Had I done something wrong in a previous lifetime? Was there some kind of lesson I needed to learn?

Shooting a quick glance at Danny, it dawned on me that he was probably the reason why we weren't getting a ride. In fact, the more I looked at Danny, the clearer it became that there… was… something… very… off… about him. While I couldn't quite put my finger on it, there was something about my so-called friend that troubled me.

"Danny," I said. "It's just not happening, bro. Let's check into a roadside motel and get a good night's sleep. Tomorrow is another day."

And so we did. And so it was. Thursday, October 4th was definitely another day. Fueled by bad hotel muffins and even worse coffee, we made our way to the now very familiar I-70 on ramp and took our positions, thumbs pointing West.

Nobody stopped. Nobody slowed down. Nobody.

"I wonder if this is what Moses was feeling in the desert," I thought to myself. True, our missions were different – him trying to get to the promised land, me trying to get to Denver, and yet, might it be true that our inner experiences were not all that different – our demons, our doubts, our dreams?

It was just about this time that Danny and I realized it probably wasn't such a good idea to be hitching *together* anymore – that the sight of two young men standing by the side of the road, might just seem a bit threatening to oncoming motorists. Like maybe we had just escaped from prison and were just about to steal their car.

So we decided to split up.

Ten minutes later a car stops and Danny gets in, waving goodbye, with a shit-eating grin on his face. I wave back, newly certain that my luck is just about to change. It doesn't. I just stand there, now a solo act. My feet hurt. My head hurts. My eyes hurt. This isn't funny anymore. OK? "Look, here's the deal, God, or whatever name you are going by these days. I NEED A RIDE BACK HOME! DO YOU HEAR ME? I NEED A RIDE. Is that too much to ask? Is it?"

And then? Like some kind of astral Clint Eastwood emerging from a dream, I see a car slow down and stop. Lo, I say unto you, the car stops. The... car... stops. Stops, as in doesn't move. Just seven feet away from me. Or maybe eight. A late model Chevy it is and, behind the wheel, a very attractive young woman. She is smiling, beckoning me to enter, pointing to the empty seat next to her.

She extends her hand and tells me her name is Lisa and, just like that, we are off. She offers me some water. She turns the music up. We talk. Fifteen minutes later, I see Danny standing by the side of the road. "STOP!" I blurt. *"That's Danny!* That's my friend Danny. STOP!"

Danny gets in and gives me a high five. We ask her where she's going and why.

"Driving west," she says, "looking for love."

That's our cue. Having just spent two days listening to the most inspiring human being we had ever encountered, the two of us let it rip, regaling her with stories of the man we had traveled cross-country to see, his message, what drew us to him in the first place, and how we felt in his presence.

Entranced, she asks us to keep on talking. We do. Then she asks us where we're going.

"Denver, Colorado," we say.

"Great, I'll take you there."

And so she does. Right to our front doors. 23 hours and 1,269 miles later.

By the time we got home, we had told her just about every story we knew – stories about love, the purpose of life, and the spiritual Master who we had just seen in Montreal. Lisa stayed in Denver for a month. There, she read everything she could find about the man we had told her about for those 23 hours. There, she watched every video of him she could get her hands on. At the end of the month, she decided to become his student and to receive the gift he called "Knowledge" – her long journey West, looking for love, now fulfilled.

FOR YOUR REFLECTION:

Back in the 15th century, it was Copernicus, the savvy Polish astronomer and mathematician, who first disavowed humanity of its long-held belief that the Earth was the center of the universe, replacing it, instead, with the sun. Copernicus, a man after who very few children are named, somehow knew that his fellow human beings' construct of reality was seriously flawed – that our planet was not at the center of things, but rather the star around which our planet revolved. And while many of us post-Copernican homo sapiens have long ago come to agree with him that the Earth is not the center of creation, we have not always understood the psychological correlative of that construct – that our so-called "selves" are not the center of the universe either, and that we, in fact, are not always the stars of our own movies.

What I experienced, standing on that Toledo on-ramp for ten hours, was a direct result of the way in which I had positioned myself in space and time – me at the center of my self-invented universe. The attachment to my desire to get back home in a time I had conceived of as "reasonable" was the belly of the whale that had swallowed me whole. The more my need to get back home was thwarted by unresponsive motorists, the more I morphed from a deeply spiritual being to "Oh, Lord, why hast thou forsaken me?" My thoughts and feelings all took shape in response to the way in which I had constructed reality. Producer and director of my own movie, I now had all the proof I needed to cast God as the boogeyman, Danny as the loser, and my own rapidly dissolving self as a victim of some kind of mysterious karma. What I didn't realize at the time was that even though I had cast myself as the star of my own movie, I was also the extra in someone else's – and that someone else, Lisa, had a storyline way more compelling than mine. Not once during my dark night of the soul experience on the Toledo on-ramp would it have ever dawned on me that a woman, in Philadelphia just beginning her journey West towards love would be the reason no one picked us up. The choreography was perfect, even if it took her 10 hours to get across the stage to the precise location where we, the other actors, stood, staring at the sky, waiting for our cue.

Time? You think you have it, but actually, it has you. On any given day none of us have the slightest clue about how long anything will take. Just because you have a goal, desire, or agenda doesn't necessarily mean it's going to happen. And the absence of it happening doesn't necessarily mean that you are the victim of karma or need to more diligently visualize the outcomes you want. Life is a play. You are in it. Sometimes you're the hero. And sometimes you're the extra.

What project of yours is taking longer than you imagined it would take? What lessons and learnings might be in this for you?

THE FISHERMAN AND THE INVESTMENT BANKER

A well-dressed investment banker, on vacation, stood at the pier of a small coastal village when a small boat docked just a few feet away. Inside the boat, a weathered fisherman stared at several large fish flopping around on the deck. Stepping closer, the investment banker complimented the fisherman on the size of his fish and asked how long it took to catch them.

"Only a little while," said the fisherman.

"Well, then," the banker asked, "why didn't you stay out longer and catch more?"

The fisherman laughed. "Why bother? I now have more than enough to feed my family."

"But what do you do with the rest of your time?" asked the investment banker.

"Let's see," said the fisherman, "I sleep late, fish a little, play with my kids, take a siesta with my wife, tend our garden, stroll into town, eat dinner, and spend some quality time with my family."

The banker frowned. "I am a Harvard MBA and can help you. You should definitely spend more time fishing. With the proceeds, you can buy a bigger boat. With the proceeds from the bigger boat, you can buy many more boats. Before you know it, you will have an entire fleet of fishing boats. Then, instead of selling your catch to a middleman who will get all the profit, you can sell directly to the processor. Eventually you can open your own cannery. Then, you will control the product, processing *and* distribution. Rich beyond your wildest dreams, you can move your family out of this Godforsaken fishing village and move to the big city. After that, who knows? Anything is possible!"

The fisherman looked up. "How long do you think all of this will take?"

"Oh, I'd say about 15 to 20 years depending on a few variables."

"But what then?" asked the fisherman.

The banker laughed, "That's the best part! When the time is right, you can announce an IPO, sell your company stock to the public, and become extremely wealthy. Millions!"

"Millions?" asked the fisherman. "Then what?"

"Then you would retire and do whatever you wanted," said the banker. *"Tell me, what would you want to do?"*

The fisherman smiled: "Well… I would sleep late, fish a little, play with my kids, take a siesta with my wife, tend our garden, stroll into town, eat dinner, and spend some quality time with my family."

FOR YOUR REFLECTION:

How can you simplify your life?

Note: The above story showed up on my Facebook feed one day. I am not sure of its origins.

AN INTRODUCTION TO BLACK MAGIC

There are a lot of things I have never been into. Biodynamic gardening is one. Shopping at Wal-Mart, is another. And black magic.

I realize, of course, biodynamic gardening has value. It's good for the earth. Shopping at Wal-Mart, I suppose, also has its advantages. Like the option of buying three months of toilet paper in one fell swoop. But black magic – *the use of supernatural powers for evil and selfish purposes?* Nope. Not my cup of tea. Not even close. Ever since I was a small boy, I've always thought of myself as one of the good guys – a light bearer, a healer, a champion of the oppressed. Black magic was as far off my radar screen as learning Swahili. But that all changed for me one rainy Tuesday night in Los Angeles, the City of Angels, in 1982.

Having just arrived from New York on a three-day business trip, a friend invited me to join him for a "different kind of evening" – an evening, he explained, with a *trance medium*, a psychic who, apparently, had the ability to channel Merlin the Magician, King Arthur's former chief advisor.

Curious, I accepted my friend's invitation and, the day after my arrival, drove to the hotel on the outskirts of town where the gathering would take place.

Not in the mood for small talk, I found a seat in the back of the room, signed no guestbook, wore no name badge, and spoke to no one. In front of me, a highly animated group of LA types talked non-stop, anticipating, it seemed, some kind of cosmic experience that awaited them. Me? I was in a different kind of mood, slipping slowly into my East Coast alter ego – "Big Vinny from Brooklyn" – the pizza-eating, wise guy nihilist with an extremely low tolerance for anything that smacked of woo woo. Let's just say that Vinny wasn't all that impressed with what he was seeing in the room.

And then, *show time* – the Merlin channel made his appearance, stage right, wearing a blue blazer, his shoes much shinier than mine. All eyes were upon him as he sat down, mumbled a few, unimpressive words of welcome, and closed his eyes. And then? He began shaking and twitching, which quickly morphed into a kind of full-body shuddering, apparently vacating the premises to make room for the 800-year-old featured speaker of the evening. When he spoke, his voice was very different than the one that had welcomed us just moments before. This one, a booming, British voice. Serious. Shakespearean. And apparently in charge. This continued for an hour or so, Merlin tuning into various members of the audience and saying things that sounded alternately profound and like a Saturday Night Live sketch.

"Bullshit!" Big Vinny screamed inside me. *"Total bullshit!"* Intermission came none too soon. I stood, made a beeline for the parking lot, found my rented Toyota, and turned on the Mets/Dodgers game. The score? 5-2. Pitching? Ron Darling, just back from three weeks on the disabled list. Bad hamstring, I think.

The New Yorker in me wanted to stay in the car, at least until the Mets took the lead. The rest of me didn't, semi-concerned that my disappearing act would seem to be a slap in the face to the friend who had invited me. And so, I begrudgingly returned to the charade.

As soon as I entered the room, I got chills up my spine. Major chills. The hairs on the back of my neck stood up. Whoa! Something had dramatically changed and I knew the second part of the evening was going to be very different than the first.

In walks the trance medium. He sits, closes his eyes, shudders, and speaks. "There's a man in the room," he announces, "who is a scientist of ideas. He knows all about white magic. But where he's going in this life, it's black magic he will need to understand. And his name is Mitchell."

OK. Badaboom, badabing. *Now* he had my attention. Everything he said was true. I was a scientist of ideas. That's what I did for a living – helping people in corporations navigate their way through the maze of their minds and originate game-changing ideas. And yes, it was also true that as a former poet, monk, and hippie, I knew a lot about white magic. *Benevolence* was my middle name, "We Are the World" was my theme song. But in the dense, patriarchal, aggressive, hyper-competitive, bottom-line focused, take-no-prisoners-world-of-corporate America I was, shall we say, just a bit over my head – Mr. Magoo at an Illuminati convention.

My approach to corporate America, up until then, had been on the light and fluffy side, a curious blend of Bodhisattva, Woody Allen, and Einstein. Black Magic was not something I noticed upon walking the halls of power, although I *did* see other things that gave me pause. Like mind games. And power plays… selfishness… greed… maneuvering… manipulation… fear… and a kind of icy cold addiction to logic that gave me the creeps. Maybe it wasn't *black magic*, per se, I was seeing, but it was definitely on the dark side of the spectrum. Like maybe grey, perhaps, or on a bad day, dark grey. Whatever color it was, one thing was clear: I was not a master at dealing with it.

The trance medium continued. More sage counsel issued forth in his booming British voice. Merlin, apparently, wasn't satisfied to merely share his 800-year old counsel with me. He also had a very specific reading list he wanted to me to know about, a bibliography of heavyweights whose books I had previously shied away from whenever frequenting a spiritual book store: Like Madame Blavatsky, for instance. And Alice Bailey. Like Ouspensky and Gurdjieff. These were not my peeps. Nor were they the peeps of my peeps. I was more a Rumi and Hafiz kind of guy, with a sprinkling of Zen Buddhism thrown in for good measure. The Mentalists? They of the furrowed brow? Too mental for me. Too heady. Too dense. Too convoluted.

I have no recollection how that evening ended. No memory of how I got back to my car or what I did later that night. All I know is I never read the books Merlin recommended. No, I did not. *But I did manage to hold them in my hands* a few weeks later and turn the pages. In a strange way that makes no sense to me, just the act of holding those books in my hands shifted something inside me that changed the way I approached my work. It was, as if, I'd been given a homeopathic dose of something or other that tweaked my sensibilities and the way I operated in the business world.

Slowly at first, and then with a steady progression, I found myself moving away from my New Age, smiley face mindset into a much more grounded one. Slowly, I began paying a different kind of attention in the marketplace. Yes, I continued seeing the good in people. And yes, I continued giving everyone the benefit of the doubt. But I didn't stop there. Goodness, indeed, was a good place to start, but it wasn't the whole story. There was shadow, too, that I needed to be mindful of. And so I started paying attention to a more subtle dimension, a kind of unspoken corporate hieroglyphics: the tilt of a head, a change of expression, the clasp of a handshake, eye contact, or the lack thereof; how long a glance was held and why, a joke, a wink, the feeling I had when someone entered the room or left, what was said; what wasn't said, and how what wasn't said wasn't said.

It was, for me, as if a veil was lifting and I began experiencing something I had either ignored or been blinded to for years. What dogs hear that their masters cannot. Not the invisible elephant in the room, but the invisible elephant behind the invisible elephant. The jealous rock 'n roll road manager skimming an extra 5% off the top while the band parties on.

For Your Reflection:

Take a moment now to think about the various scenes you are in these days, especially business scenes. Where might there be some subtle black magic going on? Or, if not black, then grey. Who might be withholding information, or trying to deceive you, or maneuvering around you in a way that doesn't feel right? What are you seeing that you would rather not see? What are you sensing? And if these questions make you uncomfortable, good. Think about them, anyway. Open your eyes. Open your mind to what is unspoken verbally, but still speaks loudly in other ways. Is there any action you need to take? *Is there something you need to do differently, going forward?*

BEYOND STAGE FRIGHT

The night before Prem Rawat's 50th birthday party event at the San Diego Convention Center, to be attended by 3,500 people, I was asked to be the MC. My response to this unexpected invitation? A curious blend of fascination and fear. *Fascination* that Prem had the confidence in me to do the job. And *fear* of totally screwing up. But since I barely had any time to prepare, I couldn't afford to indulge in freaking out. So I went to the dress rehearsal, studied the announcements, made sure my fly wasn't open, and got ready for the evening gig.

So there I am, backstage, waiting for my cue, when I am hit upside the head by the worst case of stage fright I imagine anyone, anywhere, anytime, has ever experienced. This, my friends, was well beyond anxiety or nervousness. STUCK. I was completely stuck. Frozen. Fried. Terrified. Totally in my head. I had never, in all my life, experienced such an all-encompassing sense of dread. I was the poster boy for *uptight*. Mr. Weirdo. I was so uptight, in fact, that I soon found myself praying for someone to call in a bomb scare or for the building to catch on fire – *anything* to get me out of there.

Richie, the very laidback stage manager in charge of time and space, could see I was freaking out. With just five minutes left before show time, he walked over and began giving me a shoulder massage – a kind deed that only succeeded in making things worse because now I knew, for sure, that my inner meltdown was so totally visible to the outside world that Richie, my handler, felt obliged to cool me out. Doo doo. I was in deep doo doo.

Though my body sat on a folding chair backstage, the rest of me had left for Mars. No, make that an asteroid, a very small, rocky, cold asteroid orbiting absolutely nothing.

Now there were *four* minutes to go. Now there were *three*. And there was absolutely no sign, anywhere that my hyper state of out-of-control-self-consciousness was going to abate anytime soon. This was clearly going to be the end of me. In just three minutes, everyone in the hall would know, for sure, that I was a complete idiot, a fraud and a buzz kill – someone likely to become a future synonym for the phrase "consumed with terror," as in "Hey, don't pull a Ditkoff on me."

The clock continued ticking. Now only one minute left. One minute! And then... completely out of the blue... with no warning whatsoever, two things happened that I will never forget. Not in this lifetime. And not in the next. First, on the house PA system, I heard Daya singing my favorite song, "Find the Miracle," a song that always managed to bring me back to a place of peace. The second thing? Up from the depths of my being percolated the remembrance of something I heard my teacher say many years ago, something about the choice we all have every single day of our lives.

"You can spend your entire life gritting your teeth and praying for it all to be over," he said "or you can just say YES!"

Wow! Incredible! Amazing! *I had a choice!* I could sit there in the wings, a complete and total mess or I could embrace the moment and say YES to whatever was going to happen next. So simple! A choice! I had a choice!

That's precisely the moment I said YES. And that's precisely the moment when Richie stepped forward, leaned closer, put his hand on my shoulder, and said these words: "Three... Two... One... Go!"

I stood. I took a breath. I boldly walked on stage. This wasn't the plank I was walking. This was my life! FREE! I WAS FREE! Completely free! Unshackled. Unhindered. And uncontainable! Nothing held me back. Nothing! Every ounce of who I was had become totally available to me. Everything! Whatever I needed in that timeless moment to play my part fully was fully present and accounted for. And the *feeling* behind it all was pure joy!

FOR YOUR REFLECTION:

Now I finally understand what the expression "the darkest hour is just before dawn" really means. Tell me, who of us *doesn't* battle with doubt, fear, and self-consciousness? Who *doesn't* want to run and hide when the going gets tough? Though it may not be how we want the world to see us, it comes with the territory of being human. Not just you. And not just me. All of us! But more powerful than fear is *remembrance* and the deep knowledge that we have everything we need to play our part fully in any situation. We may not feel it all the time. We may not trust it. But it's there. It is. In the end, it all comes down to choice. We can grit our teeth and pray it will all end. Or we can just say YES. *Take a moment now, to think about a seemingly difficult challenge that is fast approaching. What do you choose? Gritting your teeth or saying YES?*

MEHMET THE RUG MERCHANT

Ten years ago, my wife and I travelled to Istanbul for a three-week vacation. On the last day of our adventure we found ourselves at the Grand Bazaar, curious to see what the big deal was about this famous marketplace of more than 4,000 shops, many of which had been in the same family for 567 years. Not wanting to stand out as a tourist, I changed my accent and the way I walked as I cruised by the booths, not wanting to seem the easy mark or make eye contact with the smiling vendors standing outside their shops also trying hard to appear as if they weren't trying too hard. My wife and I were truly "just looking." We were browsers, not buyers. So we sat down at a little café and ordered two Turkish coffees and some halvah. Halfway through our afternoon repast, we noticed a middle-aged man, with a small scar over his left eye, slowly approaching our table.

"Welcome to my café," he began, in perfect English. "I trust you are finding everything to your liking?"

"Yes," I replied. "How kind of you to ask."

He just stood there, careful not to stare or seem as if he was expecting us to talk to him. And then, just before he turned to go, he mentioned that he also happened to be the owner of the rug shop just across the way, motioning to it with his hand.

"Perhaps you would be interested in visiting?" he mentioned. "I have some of the finest rugs in all of Turkey. My father, grandfather, and great grandfather were all rug merchants before me."

Though his invitation seemed genuine enough, I could feel the street-smart New Yorker in me now on high alert. "Aha!" I thought to myself, the old "give-em-Turkish-coffee-and-halvah-before-lowering-the-boom routine."

"My name is Mehmet," he said. "It is a great pleasure to meet you. Indeed, it would be my honor if you would take just a few moments to see my rugs, some of which have been made by craftsmen from the farthest regions of Turkey."

I so wanted not to like this man, to detect something so obviously off that making our departure would not only be the next logical move, but an act of great perception. Unfortunately, there was absolutely nothing not to like about him.

"Take your time," he said, with a smile. "I don't want to interrupt your meal. And if this is not a good time to visit my shop, perhaps you can return another day. Whatever day works best for you."

Gracefully, he looked off into the distance, granting my wife and I the time we needed to check in with each other. Which is what we did, then shrugged. Both of us were on the same page. Both of us were feeling the exact same thing at the exact same time: Mehmet was the real deal. The way he was relating to us was genuine, not a hustle. So we nodded, paid our bill, and followed him back to his shop. There he offered us two chairs, asked if we would like to try his favorite Turkish tea, and sent his 14-year old nephew to fetch it. For the next 45 minutes, Mehmet the Rug merchant gave us a guided tour of his world – pulling rugs off his many stacks, laying them out before us on the floor, and giving us the back story of each one: where it was made, what was unique about it, and whether or not he thought it was a good value. The man was on fire – a samurai of rugs.

My New York, street-smart, watch-out-this-might-be-a-scam guy? Gone. Try as he might to find the flaw, the fine print, and the hustle, there wasn't any. The only thing going on was Mehmet the Rug Merchant being on top of his game.

PS: We bought a rug. It is now in our dining room. Every time I walk by it, I think of Mehmet.

MEHMET'S MAGIC

1. He effortlessly established rapport.

2. He gave us all the space we needed.

3. He shared his knowledge with great feeling.

4. He had beautiful rugs and knew them better than most people know themselves.

5. He loved what he did.

6. He had a wonderful sense of humor.

7. He had kind eyes and a big heart.

8. He conducted the transaction in the spirit of service.

9. He asked us how much we thought the rug was worth and then sold it to us for less.

10. He knew what he was doing and he did it with the perfect blend of flair and humility.

FOR YOUR REFLECTION:

Take a moment to think about the way that you currently sell your product or services. If it's not going quite as well as you'd like, ask yourself: *"What can I learn from Mehmet the Rug Merchant?"*

THE SCORPION AND THE SAINT

Once a upon a time a traveling saint, on his yearly pilgrimage to the Holy Land, found himself approached by a small group of agitated villagers. He could tell by the look in their eyes that something was wrong. So he stopped, put down his begging bowl, and asked them a question: "What seems to be the problem, my friends?"

"Oh, Great Saint," the first villager began, "less than a mile from here, a powerful scorpion is terrorizing our town. Every time any one of us tries to fetch water from our lake, the scorpion attacks. His sting is painful. His poison paralyzes. Everyone in our village is filled with fear. Please, sir, can you help?"

"Hmm," replied the saint, "yours is not a good situation. Not good at all. Bring me to the place of which you speak and let me see what I can do."

And so the saint and the small band of villagers walked the distance to the lake. Ten feet from the water's edge, the villagers stopped dead in their tracks, shaking in their boots, but the saint kept on walking, wading into the water until he found himself just a few feet from the scorpion, now sunning itself on a rock.

Without a word, he lifted his arm, reached forward, scooped up the scorpion, and gently cradled it in his right hand. Immediately, the scorpion attacked, sinking his teeth into the saint's flesh. And just as immediately, the saint let go, losing control of his prey, now free to return to his perch on the rock.

A few minutes passed. Then the saint, still wincing from the sting, reached out and cradled the scorpion again, this time in his other hand. And again the scorpion attacked. And again, the saint let go and again the scorpion made his way through the water back to his perch on the rock.

This little scene continued for the rest of the day, at least 20 times, the saint reaching and the scorpion biting.

In time, the sun went down and the saint, no longer able to make out the shape of the scorpion on the rock, turned around, and made his way back to the shore.

The villagers gathered around.

"Oh great saint," the first one began, "you have our eternal gratitude for the efforts you have made today on our behalf, but with all due respect, we are confused. Each time you reached and held the scorpion in your hand, he bit you, sinking his poison into your flesh. All day you worked to rid our village of this evil menace, but no progress has been made. If you would be so kind, please explain. What kept you at your task all day?"

The saint took a long, slow breath, and looked to the sky. Then, slowly, oh so slowly, he began rubbing his hands together, again and again and again. "My friends, it is really very simple. There is nothing mysterious about what happened here today. All I was doing was fulfilling the natural order of things. You see... it is the scorpion's nature to sting. It is my nature to save."

FOR YOUR REFLECTION:

Most experienced storytellers will say the same thing about the stories they tell – that the really good ones stand on their own and need no explanation. Like Mozart's music. Or Picasso's art. Talking about a story, after it is told, they believe, runs the risk of denying listeners the chance to discover, for themselves, the deep meaning of the tale, not unlike the way political spin doctors hold forth on the nightly news, interpreting the so-called meaning of things for others.

Yes, this is true, but it is not always true. Sometimes, deconstructing a story after it's told has great value. Indeed, the act of digging into the nooks and crannies of a story often reveals the kind of insights that have the potential to change our lives for the better – the way we think, the way we feel, the way we perceive, and the way we behave – responses that increase our ability to make wise choices in the world. And it is precisely these wise choices that all of us will need to make if we expect to survive during the challenging times ahead.

Clearly, the scorpion-like nature of the obstacles upon us has never been more apparent. Terrorism, war, greed, corruption, fear, hunger, homelessness, the loss of human rights, climate change, and environmental collapse plague us – all in the midst of toxic political posturing by our so-called leaders. The proverbial plot has thickened, big time, bringing with it the need for each and every one of us, the characters in the story, to respond in ways that truly make a difference.

Our choices? Many.

Some of us choose to work within the system. We sign petitions. We call our political representatives. We meet with other concerned citizens. Others, having long ago concluded that the system is hopelessly corrupt, take it to the streets – marching, waving signs, and blocking traffic. Civil disobedience is their approach. Still others, on the far out fringes of despair, call for revolution, the complete overthrow of all existing institutions. Others, highly doubtful of their ability to have any kind of impact, choose only to vent on social media. And then, of course, there are the peacemakers – those who pray, meditate, chant, and quote from their favorite holy book, firmly believing that only a change of consciousness, not government, will make a lasting difference.

Does any of this stuff work? Of course it does. At different times, in different ways, all of it works. Not immediately. Not overnight. And not always as planned, but it works.

Is one approach better than the other? That's for you to decide, not me – a decision you will need to make very soon, as the scorpions of this world continue to take up residence all around us.

The hero of our story, the traveling saint, chose to take the high ground. He did not attack. He did not kill. He did not demonize the demon. Did his efforts succeed? At first glance, no. Nothing was resolved. At second glance? Who knows what impact his efforts made on the villagers beyond the realm of their little lake? Maybe his approach changed the way they related to their spouses or children that night. Or maybe the villagers, as a result of the saint's efforts, became more courageous, or more committed, or more tenacious in how they approached the challenges of their lives. True, at the end of the day, the scorpion wasn't dead, but maybe something else was, the villagers' unwillingness to lend a helping hand when all the odds seemed to be stacked against them.

I am not suggesting that you should become more like the saint. I am not suggesting you take the "spiritual path" and love thy scorpion as thyself. All I'm suggesting is that you pause by the water's edge and ask yourself one simple question: *What is my responsibility?* When facing seemingly insurmountable odds, when your back is up against the wall, when there is no easy solution, what choice will you make?

YOU – part villager, part saint, part scorpion – what is your path forward during these days of upheaval and unrest? What will you do to make a difference? *What efforts will you make to help relieve the suffering in the world? And what is your next step?*

HOW 13-YEAR-OLD GIRLS CAN WIPE OUT TERRORISM

OK. I know this headline seems bold. Even presumptuous. But bear with me. I'm inspired. And even more than that, on the brink of a breakthrough. But first, a bit of back story.

Eight years ago, my awesomely cool, smart, and creative daughter, Mimi, turned 13 and invited 12 of her girlfriends to our house for a celebrational sleepover. The first 30 minutes were great as each girl, gift in hand, was dropped off by a parent, who, upon surveying the room, offered my wife and I a glance of great compassion as if to say, "Better you than me."

The girls? Don't ask. They talked. They texted. They talked. They texted. Ate chocolate. Brushed hair. Played music. Painted fingernails. Laughed. Texted. Called friends. Finished not a single sentence, rolling their eyes every time a parent entered the room.

Mindful of my daughter's need for space and my own weird tendency to be a little too present when her friends were around, I retreated to my bedroom like some kind of midwestern chicken farmer looking for a storm shelter. I tried reading. I tried napping. I tried meditating. Nothing worked, my attention subsumed by a vortex of social networking energy channeled by a roomful of partying 13-year old girls. I felt dizzy, confused, beside myself. And then, with absolutely no warning, everything became suddenly clear. In a flash, I understood exactly how to end terrorism once and for all.

For starters, the government flies a squadron of 13-year-old girls to Guantanamo or wherever high profile terrorists are being interrogated these days. The girls, impeccably guarded by the highest qualified soldiers available, are walked into a prison waiting room where the shackled terrorists are already sitting.

Immediately, the girls begin texting, eating chocolate, talking, painting fingernails, and exponentially interrupting each other with a steady stream of OMG's and other esoteric internet acronyms none of their parents understand.

The prisoners, at first, find the whole thing amusing, a delightful break from their dreadful prison routine. They smile. They wink. They remember their youth. But the girls, wired to the max (sugar and Wi-Fi), radically pick up the pace of their texting and talking like some kind of futuristic teenage particle accelerator. After five minutes, the prisoners stop smiling. After ten, they become silent. After 20, they start twitching. A lot. They try covering their ears with their shackled hands, but the chains are too short. They start looking madly around the room, hoping to catch the eyes of their jailers, but their jailers sit motionless, miming the movements of the 12 texting teenagers. A few of the terrorists start crying. A few go catatonic. And then, the roughest looking of the bunch, a tall man with a long, jagged scar on his left cheek, calls out in his native language.

"STOP! I CAN'T TAKE IT ANYMORE! I'll TELL YOU EVERYTHING YOU WANT TO KNOW!"

The guards nod and switch on the nearest tape recorder. But it's unnecessary. The girls, totally tuned into the terrorists' confessions, as if watching the finals of "American Idol," are texting everything they hear to a roomful of Pentagon heavyweights in an undisclosed location. The information proves vital to our national defense. Within three days, a record number of terrorist cells are taken down. Word gets out to the global terrorist community and, in only a matter of weeks, it becomes impossible for the Jihadist movement to recruit.

Yes, of course, the ACLU raises a stink about this "new strain of American torture," but a thorough investigation by a bi-partisan task force of international peacekeepers proves to be inconclusive. No long-term damage to the prisoners can be detected.

On a roll, my daughter and her rock-the-world friends create a Facebook Group that teaches other 13-year-old girls how to help the cause. A movement is born. Soon, hundreds of teenage-girl patriots are dispatched to war zones around the world, radically decreasing the incidence of terrorism on all seven continents. Subsequent interviews with former Jihadists reveal that merely the threat of being in a room with 12 texting 13-year old girls was enough to get them to lay down their homemade bombs and return to farming.

Peace comes to the Middle East. Pakistan and India make up. (Make up, girls!) The Golden Age begins. As you might guess, HBO and Hollywood come calling. Big-time producers want to do a reality show and a major motion picture, but the girls, newly inspired by the impact they've had on the world, refuse to become a commodity as they prepare (OMG!) for summer camp and 8th grade and the September launch of that next, cool cell phone with the incredible keyboard.

FOR YOUR REFLECTION:

"What is the simplest, funniest, or strangest idea you have for establishing world peace?"

THE TRUE FRUIT OF THE SPIRITUAL PATH

Every spiritual tradition in the world has its own collection of rites and rituals that make up the warp and woof of its particular path. These rites and rituals, the origins of which are not necessarily understood, give its practitioners something to do, something not just to think about or to meditate on, but a physical activity to engage in that helps them connect more readily to the metaphysical essence of their spiritual path.

I get it. I do. Rituals work. Or as my rabbi liked to say, "If you want to learn to dance, sometimes you need to start with the box step."

My kids, for example, cannot celebrate Christmas without leaving milk and cookies out for Santa, even though it's been years since they realized that the fat guy in the red suit didn't have a snowball's chance in hell of making it down our chimney.

While I have never been a big fan of rites and rituals, I definitely have experienced their benefit, the most memorable one happening for me in 1974. That was the year I lived in a spiritual commune, on a 600-acre farm, 12 miles outside of Charlottesville, Virginia. Three times each week, the six of us would sit cross-legged in our living room and share from the heart – part of a commonly agreed upon spiritual practice.

It was at one of these gatherings that I first heard the news about an ashram that would soon be moving to our little town. An ashram! A center of spiritual life! A divine abode of God-seeking souls, students of my teacher's who had dedicated their lives to the realization of the highest truth. I couldn't believe my good fortune. Now I would have a place to go and serve whenever I wanted to dive deeper into the heart of my spiritual path. Cool. Very cool.

Back then, as I understood it, the prevailing ritual of welcoming a new ashram to one's town was to bring a gift, usually a flower or a piece of fruit, and place it, with great love, on the altar. And so, on the ashram's opening day, I made a pilgrimage to my favorite grocery store in search of the perfect piece of fruit.

The cantaloupes looked great, but seemed a tad too big to place upon an altar. The apples also looked great. They were red, unblemished, and shiny. Too shiny, I thought, almost as if they had been polished in some back room to make them stand out. Uh Uh. No way did I want my offering to stand out. I wanted my offering to fit in with the other flowers and fruit. Hey, this wasn't about me and my offering. This was about selfless giving, right? That's when I noticed the oranges, perfectly round, unpolished, and delicately textured pieces of fruit. Yes! Oranges!

Choosing the roundest and most orangey orange I could find, I blissfully made my way through the Five Items Or Less check-out lane, carefully positioned my orange on the passenger seat of my 1966 Volkswagen, and began driving to the ashram — a destination that would soon become the radiant sun around which the Pluto of my longing revolved.

Driving more slowly than usual to ensure my orange didn't roll onto the floor, I closed my eyes and meditated at every traffic light and stop sign. Beauty was everywhere. The dogwood trees were blooming. The robins were singing. And the sweetest of fragrances filled the air.

And then, just as I turned the corner, as if choreographed by the hand of an all-knowing God, the perfect parking space opened up right in front of my destination. How fortunate I was! How graced! I closed my eyes and meditated some more.

Five minutes passed. Then another five. If there was one thing I knew for sure it was this: my front-seat meditation wasn't going to be of the token "minute of silence" variety. Nope. No way. My meditation would be the real deal, as real as the feeling that brought me here in the first place.

Lovingly lifting my orange into the air, inspecting it for dust and dirt, I made my way out of the car, ascended a few steps, and walked the last few feet to the front door. Pausing briefly, I took a long slow breath and rang the bell. What a sweet sound it was, a chime for the ages. And then, just as the sound slowly faded into the distance, I enjoyed an even sweeter silence. A few seconds passed. Then the door opened. Standing there was a hairy, pot-bellied man in a stained undershirt. He had a bottle of beer in his left hand.

"Yeah?" he said, "whaddya want?"

"Um... er... is this...uh... the ashram?" I asked.

"Hell no!" he barked. "Those freaks don't move in until tomorrow." Then he slammed the door in my face. I just stood there, unmoving, a perfectly round orange in my right hand.

FOR YOUR REFLECTION:

What spiritual concepts have you had in your life? How did they serve you at the time? *And what changed for you as you let these concepts go?*

IS THAT SO?

Once upon a time, many years ago, before the invention of Starbucks, Velcro, or fructose, there lived a humble monk in a remote monastery in China. His name was Wan Lu, a man much beloved by everyone he met, dedicated as he was to realizing the highest truth with every fiber of his being.

Every morning, he meditated with the other monks in the Central Hall, then ate breakfast, washed his bowl, and worked in the garden for the rest of the day, taking brief moments now and again to read the sutras and teach calligraphy to the younger monks. Life was simple for Wan Lu. And very fulfilling. He couldn't have imagined a better life.

One day, in the 17th year of his monastic life, while cultivating radishes in the upper garden, the venerable Abbot approached him along with three of the local townspeople – a husband, wife, and their very pregnant 16-year old daughter.

"That's him!" the girl cried out, pointing to the monk, "He's the one who did this to me! Him!"

Wan Lu, still weeding the radishes, looked up slowly, smiled, and uttered just three words: "Is that so?"

And with that, the Abbot, a stern expression on his face, began to speak. "It is time for you to leave the monastery, Wan Lu. It is time! You have broken one of our most sacred vows. Now go!"

And just like that, Wan Lu had to leave the only home he had ever known.

For the next five years, he lived in a small hut far away from the monastery. Each day he woke at 4:00 AM, meditated, and, from dawn to dusk, dug graves in a nearby cemetery to make the money to buy milk for the little boy the people of the region had come to call "the young monk's son."

Wan Lu continued with his life. He never complained. He never took a day off. And he never stopped meditating.

Then, one summer day, in the fifth year of his exile, while cultivating a few tomato plants just outside his hut, he looked up and saw the young girl, her parents, the Abbot, and the now five-year old boy all standing over him.

"Oh, mother and father," began the young girl, in between tears. "The time has come for me to speak the truth. It was not the monk. It was a boy I met in the fish market. He is the father of my son – not the monk."

Big silence. Big, big silence. No one spoke. The young monk just sat there, looking up, a ripe tomato in his left hand.

"Is that so?" he said.

FOR YOUR REFLECTION:

In what ways are you being falsely accused or judged by others – especially the people closest to you? How does it make you feel? *And what, if anything can you do, to maintain your own center even as others project their negative thoughts?*

THE DREAM LETTER

Stories, like air and most people's discomfort with their driver's license photo, are an omnipresent phenomenon. Stories are everywhere, even in our dreams. Deconstruct any dream and you will find story, the narrative that our subconscious mind conceives even while we attempt to do nothing but sleep. Yes, our body might be resting, but our mind is not, continuing the saga of our life on planet Earth (and who knows where else) – new stories being told without us even trying. We are late night scribes, it seems, inheritors of tales that need to be told, at least to ourselves. What follows is a story I dreamed, one night, at the beginning of my relationship to the woman who is now my wife. That was 26 years ago, but the story, deeply embedded in my cells, continues to reveal its meaning to me.

The scene opens with Evelyne and I in what seems to be a classroom at her guru's ashram. We are both sitting behind wooden desks, which are neatly arranged behind a number of other desks, all in rows. Each of us are handed "test books" so we can write our answers to a question that has not yet been asked. I look to my right where Evelyne is sitting and notice that her test book looks very different than mine. Hers is an elegantly bound brown leather tome with embossed designs on the cover. As she turns the pages, I can see that each one contains a line of Sanskrit, with room below to write the answers.

Mine is a plain-looking "blue book," the kind my college professors used to hand out before exams. It is bound together with staples and there's a place for my name on the cover.

The topic we are being asked to write about? "The Motherhood and Fatherhood of God." That's it. Nothing else. There is no fine print beneath that sentence, no word length, no time limit. Just "The Motherhood and Fatherhood of God." That's it.

I open my book to begin writing, but notice there's a piece of paper in the front of it – one with all the answers on it. But I don't want anyone else's answers. So I raise my hand and someone comes to take the answer page away so I can write my own. As I do, I notice, that Evelyne's guru has begun to slowly descend a staircase – one I cannot see from where I'm sitting. I continue watching. Twenty seconds later she reappears, holding, in her right hand, a glass with some green powder on the bottom. Then she fills the glass with water and hands it to me to drink. I do. Then I complete my test.

The next thing I know, I am being handed a sealed envelope with Evelyne's test scores in it. On the back are two words. Just two: "Support Evelyne."

Then the scene changes. I am standing in a forest. It is green, dense, and very ancient. I am alone. There are no paths, no signposts, and no one to ask for directions. Letter in hand, I begin walking. Off in the distance, I see the vague outline of what seems to be a hut. I keep walking until I arrive. I do not knock. I just turn the doorknob and enter.

In front of me, to my left, I see a wooden staircase, going up, its stairs well-worn. To my right, I see six young men, who I assume to be some kind of security force. Thin, pale, and quiet, they seem to be yogis. All I am doing is standing there, letter in hand. I glance at these men and they glance at me. Their thoughts, which I can read, are telling me to stop, but there is no power in them, no conviction, no life. It was as if they are performing some kind of ritual they don't completely understand. The more I look at them, the more I see they are not really yogis at all – only New Age, suburban pretenders, trying too hard to be holy. I walk past them without a word and ascend the staircase. At the top, there is a room, a small room, some kind of sanctuary, it seems. Evelyne is standing in the middle of it, waiting. I walk forward and hand her the letter. Then I wake up.

FOR YOUR REFLECTION:

Some spiritually minded people, including a whole bunch of Australian aborigines, claim the world is just a dream – that it's not real, even if the dream seems real. Lao Tzu, the great Chinese sage once dreamed he was a butterfly, but confessed to not knowing whether he was a man dreaming he was a butterfly or a butterfly dreaming he was a man. If there's anything certain, it's this: nothing is certain. Oh, and one more thing: the stories we dream, conceive, and tell are our best attempt at making sense of our experiences. Are they real? Yes, if we believe them. Can they be interpreted differently? Of course they can. Does that mean your life is a dream? Or, perhaps more accurately, does it mean that you are dreaming your life and then telling stories to help make sense of your dream? Who knows? The fact is: you have a choice about what stories to conceive and what stories to tell. *What is the most memorable dream you have ever had and who might benefit from your sharing it with them?*

THE ONLY HIT OF THE SEASON

There are entire years of my life I can barely remember, but I will never forget the *nanosecond*, as a 14-year old right fielder for Camp Scatico, when I got my only hit of the season.

It was a bullet up the middle, right through the pitcher's legs, over second base, and into center field before you could say "Duke Snider." Bam! It was a perfect hit. Seriously. A major crack of the bat. A single for the ages. Pete Rose-like. Derek Jeter-like. Tony Gwynn-like. There were two outs at the time and my best friend, Matt, our rather over-sized catcher, stood on second. As soon as I made contact, Matt was off and running, heading to third, *lumbering*, as most catchers do, not all that quickly. Me? I sprinted out of the batter's box and got to first in a flash, stunned that I now had a batting average and had earned the right to stand on first base and take it all in – the *glory*, the accomplishment, the sense of timeless *connection* to all of the lead-off hitters since the beginning of time. "Speedsters" we were called. "Table setters."

But Matt got thrown out at home! Truly. I shit you not. My only chance for an RBI the entire season got gunned down at home by the maniac centerfielder, who must have been a relative of Roberto Clemente. Yup. Big Matt got thrown out. It wasn't even close. He was out by 15 feet. And it was the *third* out, at that. Third out, as in end of the inning. Finito. Kaput. No, I was not allowed to stand on first base and admire my handiwork. No, there weren't even a few seconds to accept high fives from the first-base coach. The inning was over. Done. End of story. Now I had to run back to the dugout, find my glove, and make my way out to right field.

I can barely remember my first marriage. I have no memory of high school geometry. I cannot tell you what I ate for breakfast this morning. But I remember absolutely everything about that summertime at-bat 56 years ago. *Everything*.

Did I mention it was my only hit of the season, a single up the middle, through the pitcher's legs and over second base before anyone could even blink? That's how hard I hit the ball. I mean, it literally *rocketed* off my bat. And I sprinted to first. *Sprinted*. And the crowd went wild. Totally wild. And my good buddy, Matt "I'm-Not-Exactly-Usain Bolt" Weinstein, GOT THROWN OUT AT HOME! THROWN OUT! TO END THE INNING! YOU CAN ASK ANYONE!

It wasn't funny then, but it is very funny now.

This is precisely how I want to live my life, ladies and gentlemen. One swing of the bat! *Contact! Major contact!* And I am running, like a man on fire, to first base, enjoying the moment for as long as I can, no matter what happens next. Or doesn't. PLAY BALL!

For Your Reflection:

What one moment in your life will you remember forever, even if it was "no big deal." *What message came in that moment? What does it still have to teach you? And who might you share this story with today?*

SELMA SPEAKS

My mother, Sylvia, was a quintessential Jewish mother. She played canasta. She ate bagels. She got her hair done once a week. And, knock on wood and spit three times, she thought I could do no wrong. That is, until 1971, when I received Knowledge from that "boy guru," known at the time as "Maharaji." Bottom line, my mother had no way to relate to the whole thing. First of all, Maharaji *wasn't Jewish*. Second of all, he was from India. And third of all, see reasons #1 and #2.

Of course, my over-the-top proclamations about Knowledge and my new teacher's apparent perfection didn't help matters in the least. Nor did my sudden habit of lighting incense in my parent's home. It wasn't enough that my girlfriend wasn't Jewish (a shiksa!), now I had an *Indian guru*. As they say in the old country, "Oy Vey."

All of which led my mother, one fine spring day, to forbid me, *for all time*, from ever speaking about "the guru" in her home.

"No problem, Ma," I replied, affecting my best suburban yogi's attempt at being *non-attached*. "Mum's the word."

Five years passed. Life was good. I was happy. And my adolescent need to convince my parents of anything had vanished. Then I got word that Maharaji was coming to Miami for a weekend event, one I absolutely wanted to attend. This, I figured, my parents didn't really need to know, so I simply told them I was flying in to visit them on Sunday, not wanting to push their buttons.

As usual, when the Jewish, golden-boy, prodigal son returns home, his parents invite as many of their friends as possible to celebrate his return. All the regulars were there: Blanche, Shirley, Ellie, Irv, Bert, Seymour, Solly, and a few new friends I hadn't yet met. Taking a deep breath, I knocked on the door and let myself in, surveying the room and enjoying that sweet moment of arrival, just before the slightly deflating reality of visiting one's parents truly sinks in. An elderly Jewish woman in the back of the room, someone I had never met before, stood up, waved, and smiled at me.

"Oy gevalt, Mitchell," she said. "*Wasn't Maharaji beautiful? I could have plotzed!*"

Little did I know she was also a student of this young Master. I looked at my mother. My mother looked at me.

"Hey, Ma," I said, shrugging. "She's your friend. *I didn't say a thing.*"

For Your Reflection:

This story can easily be dismissed as a moment of comic relief and nothing else, a cute scene from a Seinfeld show. And while it is true that the story's punch-line is, indeed, a funny one, there is something else going on beneath the surface. Carl Jung summarized this something else in just four words. "What you resist, persists." You see, my mother was deeply disturbed by my choice to become a student of a young Indian Master. It did not fit her paradigm. And because it didn't, she laid down the law. But while she may have been able to silence me, she wasn't able to silence one of her best friends – a woman who my mother had no idea was also a student of the same Master. Simply put, *what my mother resisted, persisted* – and it was the manifestation of this persistence that was so funny. My question to you? *What hard-to-comprehend choice made by a family member – a choice you have dismissed as ignorant, foolish, or immature – might you need to reconsider?*

THE LONG DISTANCE DELI MAN

Some years ago, in a bold attempt to ensure the future success of the innovation consulting company I co-founded, my business partner and I decided to take our entire staff away for a day of teambuilding in the wilds of Colorado. Everybody was psyched, thrilled at the chance to get out of the office and learn, through hands-on experience, what it would take for us to become a high-performing team.

The night before our adventure, we met at a fancy restaurant in Boulder to kick things off. Many glasses of wine were imbibed. Many stories were told. Many hugs and high fives were exchanged. When it was time for dessert, I went around the table, person by person, and took lunch orders for the next day. My goal? To place our orders first thing in the morning so I could pick them up on our way out of town.

The next morning, bleary-eyed from the previous evening's celebration, the 14 of us gathered in the deli parking lot to figure out who would be travelling in which cars. I took the opportunity to make my way to the deli counter and pick up our food for the day: 14 sandwiches, 14 bags of chips, and a whole bunch of soda, health drinks, and water. The owner of the deli, a pleasant enough man with a poorly drawn tattoo of an eagle on his left arm, handed me four bags of food and drink, asked me where we were headed, and wished me a good day. So far, so good.

It was only an hour later, halfway to our destination, when I realized I'd left everyone's lunch on the deli counter back in Boulder. I had paid for it, yes, but then forgotten to transport it to the car. Turning back was out of the question. We couldn't afford to tack on another two hours to our day. Nor did we have time to stop on the road to buy food. The contract I'd signed with the teambuilding facility had made it abundantly clear that if we were more than 30 minutes late, our reservation would be cancelled. Oh, I almost forgot, there were no restaurants or grocery stores where we were headed. Only a few vending machines.

Too embarrassed to let anyone know about our predicament, I said nothing. All I did, upon arriving, was approach the front desk to let the owner know we were there. He smiled, bent low, stood again to his full height, and placed four bags of food on the counter between us – the same four bags I had left behind, in the Boulder deli, just 90-minutes ago.

Then he leaned in closer and spoke: "Dude, the deli guy noticed you'd left your sandwiches behind. So he got in his car five minutes after you left and beat you here. I'm guessing he must have passed you on the highway."

FOR YOUR REFLECTION:

What the Boulder deli man did that day, I will never forget. For want of a better phrase, let's just call it *going beyond the call of duty*. The man actually left his place of business, got in his car, and drove 90 minutes to a remote location in the boonies of Colorado to deliver our lunch. And he didn't even stay around for us to thank him. Did he have to do this? No. Would I have been disappointed if he hadn't done this? No, again. Driven by an extraordinary impulse to go the extra mile (or, in his case, 90 extra miles) that's exactly what he did. Twenty-five years later I still think about what the Boulder deli man taught me that day. The food he delivered fed my team and me for a day, but the story born out of this experience has fed thousands of people for years. And now, you get to eat...

What can you do this week to go "beyond the call of duty?" In what ways can you go the extra mile to delight someone in a way they will never forget?

WHAT HAVE YOU ACCOMPLISHED TODAY?

As I gear up to enter my eighth decade on planet Earth, I find myself at a curious crossroads, the intersection of *who and what*, one of those strange intersections far out of town where the sagebrush rolls and the GPS signal is faint. Sitting in the front seat of my leased 2015 Honda, wondering how I gained the last five pounds, I ask myself a question highly unlikely to gather a crowd: "Have I done anything of significance these past 69 years?"

It's an age-old dilemma, methinks, a classic bout of rite-of-passage, the time when a man takes stock of himself and realizes his so-called "portfolio" of accomplishments doesn't necessarily measure up to what he imagined it would one day. And while I have always felt a breathtaking magnificence inside me, *outwardly* much of what I have expressed seems to have been lost in translation – not unlike the children's game of

Telephone where you whisper something to the person next to you and they, in turn, whisper it to the person next to them and so on and so forth around the circle until the last person blurts out what they've heard – a jumble of words not even remotely close to those that started the whole game.

A few months shy of 70, focused more today on the butterflies in my stomach than the ones that herald spring, I find myself looking in two directions at once – forward, toward how to best live the time I have left *and* backwards, trying to make sense of the forces that have brought me to this moment in time.

Behind me, I see my father coming home from a long day's work. He's exhausted, unsettled, my mother greeting him with a martini and the officiousness of a 50s housewife, me tentatively approaching, receiving a quick hug and the all-too-familiar question: *"What have you accomplished today?"* – a kind of Zen koan that always left me feeling like I hadn't done enough. Yes, I played roofball and punchball and kickball and stickball that day. And yes, I played with my dog and read the backs of my baseball cards. But did I *accomplish* anything? Did I really do anything that mattered?

The older I got, the more my father's accomplishment mantra embedded its way into my psyche, a kind of microscopic parasite that a person might pick up on a brief trip to a third-world country. And though I couldn't see it, I could *feel* it – radiating outwards, driving me to do, do, do – moving me to create something, which I considered significant. Clearly, there was *something* I hadn't yet accomplished, something of import, but what?

My friends, I think it is time for me (and maybe, you, too) to answer that all-too-familiar question. Ready? *"What have you accomplished today?"* In the spirit of Lao Tzu, here is the answer: NOTHING!

"The foolish man," explained the great Master, "is always doing yet much remains to be done. The wise man does nothing, yet nothing remains undone."

Capiche? There is nothing to do! There is no place to go! There is nothing to prove! Unless you and I can live in this space of nothingness, our life will never be more than our programmed/neurotic/obsessive attempt to achieve – the carrot dangled in our direction by the collective hallucination that we have never really done enough. Of course, the *opposite* is also true: While nothing matters, so does everything.

Here's how I see it: There is absolutely nothing we can do that will ever be enough compared to the outcome we imagine it should be. Maybe this is why Van Gogh cut off his ear or countless creative souls drink too much, think too much, and eventually wonder why they didn't go into their father's business. You see, the obsession with proving our worth via our creative endeavors is a losing game. First of all, the self does not need to be proven. It is already complete just the way it. And second of all, there is no second of all. The bottom line? THIS is the moment. What you do is way less important than how you do it. Living is the key. Not making a living. When you tell your stories from that place, everything makes sense.

FOR YOUR REFLECTION:

What is really important to you in this life – above and behind making a living? *At the end of the day, what do you think really matters? Any stories in there you want to tell about this?*

THE SANCTUARY WITHIN

There are three kinds of storytelling in the world: oral, written, and visual. Of the three, oral storytelling is the most common, having been around since the beginning of time. That's how our ancestors ensured their survival and passed on their wisdom to the next generation.

In time, oral storytelling morphed into written storytelling – not exclusively, of course, but as simply another way to convey vital information and share wisdom. In the 1800s, for example, two brothers in Germany collected more than 200 folk tales from their homeland and published them in a book we know as *Grimm's Fairy Tales*. In the process, however, the two brothers, Jacob and Wilhelm, edited the stories quite a bit, according to their own values, and the stories changed.

This is not at all surprising. All stories morph when told and retold. Stories constantly change, based on the memory, mood, personality, interpretation, values, and the communication style of the storytellers who tell them.

The facts upon which a story is based? Changing all the time. And that is not a problem. Because storytelling, as a communication medium, is less about *accuracy* than it is about *meaning*. Indeed, as Frank Lloyd Wright once said, "the truth is more important than the facts."

And so, dear storyteller-in-waiting, know this: As long as you are not in a court of law vowing to "tell the truth, the whole truth, and nothing but the truth," it is perfectly fine to tell a story you've heard (or read) in a different way than how you originally heard or read it. That is, as long as you honor the underlying message of the story. You see, your main service as a storyteller is bringing to water to the thirsty. The shape of the container is secondary.

In the spirit of the Grimm Brothers and millions of storytellers since the beginning of time, it is my great privilege, now, to share a story I heard, three years ago, in Mexico, from a tour guide named "Carlos," one of the most animated storytellers I have ever encountered. The story Carlos told me blew my mind so completely that I felt certain it must be a famous story written down somewhere. It wasn't. Googling revealed nothing except a few icy cold, biographical facts about the story's hero – none of which remotely sparked the power and glory of the tale I was told.

Can I say with 100% assurance that Carlos's telling of the tale was a perfect recounting of historical facts? No, I cannot. But for the purpose of your own future storytelling, it doesn't matter in the least. What matters is the message embedded *within* your stories and the impact they have on the people who have the good fortune to receive them.

Ready?

In the 18th century, in the heart of Mexico, there lived a small group of priests in service to Jesus Christ. Like most men of the cloth, these priests had a hierarchy – an organizational structure that helped them get things done. The eldest were the organizers and decision makers. The youngest took their orders from the eldest. One of the younger priests, an especially animated young man named Felipe, troubled his superiors because he was always asking questions, looking up to the sky, and he wore an unexplainable smile on his face most of the time. He was, in a phrase, a thorn in the elders' side, serious fellows who were always, it seemed, more interested in the letter of the law than the spirit.

And so, one day, the elder priests hatched a plan to get Felipe out of their hair. With great gravitas, they called him into their office and explained that he had been selected, out of all the priests, to perform a very important religious function – one that would honor the life and teachings of Lord Jesus Christ himself.

Every day, the priests explained, Felipe would be given a large wooden cross to carry for a distance of many miles into the wilderness. Upon arriving, his task would be to stop, pray, and then make his way back to where he had started that day. His journey, the priests went on to explain, would be a re-enactment of what Jesus had endured and would help Felipe and, by extension, all the priests of his order, get more deeply in touch with God. Of course, to the head priests, this exercise was nothing more than a ruse to get rid of Felipe for the day. But for Felipe, it was a gift from God. He was ecstatic that he had been chosen and couldn't wait to begin.

And so he did. Each day he would pick up his cross and walk for what seemed like forever into the wilderness – just him, his mission, and the hot sun overhead. A lesser man might have collapsed under the weight of the cross and the seeming monotony of this spiritual practice. But not Felipe. He loved it, gaining strength and inspiration with each passing day.

Two weeks into his adventures, a band of breast-plated Spaniards on horseback approached him, having noticed his daily cross-carrying ritual and the undeniable fact that, unlike them, he had never once been attacked by the Chichimeca, a ferocious indigenous tribe that had been picking off the Spaniards, one-by-one, and decimating their numbers.

The Spaniards had a deal to make with Felipe. Each day they would give him a few gold and silver coins if he would protect them from the Chichimecas – a deal that sounded to Felipe as if it was coming straight from God, especially since he recently had a vision of building a church in the wilderness and had no idea how he was going to pay for materials. And so, he accepted the Spaniards' offer, using most of his sudden good fortune to pay for building supplies, giving the rest of the gold and silver to the priests when he returned home at the end of each day.

And so it went. Months passed. Years. The priests got richer and Felipe's church grew taller. All was right with the world. Except one thing. The lack of water in the region made it impossible for Felipe and his indigenous helpers to build the church year-round. With no water to make adobe bricks, they were forced to wait for months until the rainy season began – not an ideal scenario for a man on a mission, a cross on his back, and a constant smile on his face.

A problem? Not to Felipe. Guided by unseen forces and his trusty divining rod, he soon discovered an underground spring nearby. With nothing but his bare hands, a few primitive implements, and his Chichimecan helpers, Felipe dug until they found water. Not just any water, however. *Mineral water.* Healing water. The kind of water that people travel hundreds of miles to bathe in.

Now, with no more need to wait for the rainy season to begin, Felipe and his helpers moved into high gear and, in time, completed their project – a beautiful, hand-built church, made with love, a testament to the power of love, faith, collaboration, and fearless dedication.

Imagine, if you will, the look on the faces of the priests who had originally sent Felipe into the wilderness, when they joined him one fine spring day on his cross-carrying walk. There, rising up from the ground in the distance, rose the church now known as the Sanctuary of Atotonilco – the church Felipe had painstakingly built with his own two hands and the help of others drawn to his mission – a glorious testament to faith and virtue, built one brick at a time, in service to God and the transformative power of love.

Today, the Sanctuary of Atotonilco is a World Heritage site, a sacred destination for as many as 5,000 people per week who come to pray and do penance. And some of these pilgrims, the lucky ones, get to listen to Carlos the Tour Guide tell the story of the priest who found God by leaving his place of worship each day, cross on his back, to build one of his own.

FOR YOUR REFLECTION:

What does it mean to be a man or woman of God? Who knows? Different people will answer this question in different ways. But everyone can agree on the power of story to provide the kind of pregnant pause to consider the question in the first place. The story of Felipe, I am sure, has gone through hundreds of changes since the first time it was told – each storyteller making it his or her own. The version Carlos told me is not exactly the one I have just told. And if you decide to retell this tale, it will undoubtedly change again. So be it. Such is life. The facts and details of the story may change, but the wisdom *embedded* within it will remain the same – a single, inspired human being can make a profound difference; love, faith, and perseverance are three of the most powerful forces in the world; and surrendering to one's true purpose can work miracles against all odds.

FIVE FEET OFF THE GROUND

Many centuries ago after years of wandering alone in the forests of India, a young seeker of truth found himself, hungry, thirsty, and exhausted, at the entrance of the most remote ashram in the land. Gathering whatever strength he had left, he knocked on the ashram's massive wooden door and asked the gatekeeper for shelter, a request granted, under one condition – at sunrise, he must be on his way.

Thrilled at his good fortune, the young man agreed to the condition and was immediately escorted to a room with a mat on the floor, a tray of food, and a faded photo of a bearded man whom he assumed was the resident guru.

Sleep came easy to him that night, grateful as he was for a good meal and a chance to rest his weary bones. And rest he did. Deeply. Very deeply. That is, until the door to his room swung wildly open and there, standing just a few feet away, holding a small candle, loomed the man in the faded photo.

"Stand up!" he commanded. *"Stand up and follow me. We don't have much time."*

And with those twelve words, the Master turned and exited – the young seeker doing all he could to follow closely behind. Outside, a violent storm raged. Lightning crackled. Thunder boomed. The wind and the rain were relentless.

For an hour they walked, deeper and deeper into a forest, the young seeker having no clue where they were going or why. And then, without warning, at the foot of a gigantic tree, the Master stopped, turned, and uttered a single word. "Climb!"

The young seeker, sensing the revelation of timeless teaching, grabbed the lowest branch, pulled himself up, and began his ascent – a far from easy task. Not tonight. Not in this darkness. And not in this storm. Still, he persevered, branch-by-branch, handhold-by-handhold, breath-by-breath, his perilous pathway up illuminated only by occasional flashes of lightning.

How long he climbed, no one knows. Nor does anyone know how many times he almost lost his balance and fell to what would have surely been certain death. The only thing known for sure is that in time he made it to the top, and, upon arriving, raised both his arms to the heavens in a bold salute to victory against all odds.

And then, just a few seconds later, wind continuing to howl, he began his descent, an effort far more difficult than his ascent, his muscles now fatigued, his hands cramped and raw, the massive tree swaying precariously in the wind.

An hour passed. And then, when he had finally managed to reach the lowest branch, just five feet off the ground, the Master let out a ferocious roar. "WATCH OUT!" he screamed. "WATCH OUT!!!!!"

Stunned, the young lad simply hopped down, stood to his full height, and approached the Master.

"Oh Enlightened One," he began, "please forgive my ignorance, but I am totally confused. All during my ascent, through the rain and the wind, through the lightning and thunder, you said nothing to me – not a single word. Many times, I was almost blown off the tree and yet you remained silent. The same held true for my descent, an even more difficult task. Not once did you issue a word of caution. Not once did you advise or encourage me. But *now*, just five feet off the ground, you shout your warning? This makes no sense, no sense at all."

"Precisely, my son. Precisely! All during your ascent, you knew in your bones just how dangerous the conditions were – and because you did, you hung on for dear life. No words of caution were necessary. In fact, my words would have only distracted you from your mission. And the same held true for your descent. You knew, as you made your way down, what the challenge was. Ah… but just *five feet off the ground*, when you assumed your work was done, that was the time of greatest danger. That is when you could have been injured, which is why I spoke. Know this, my friend, the most dangerous time is always just before completion.

FOR YOUR REFLECTION:

All of us, at some point in our lives, have committed to a difficult task imbued with great meaning and purpose for us – a goal not easy to achieve. Maybe no one else knew of our adventures and the obstacles that stood in our way, but we did. We knew the path forward was not an easy one. We knew that we would need to rise to the occasion in a big way. If this describes you, know that you have also had your *climbing-a-tree-in-the-middle-of-a-raging-storm* moment and also your tree descent moment – the time when all of the forces within you needed to be marshaled. Just like the young seeker who was awakened from a deep sleep and asked to accomplish the seemingly impossible, you too have being called – or are being called now. You, too, no matter how much effort you've expended, have found yourself five feet off the ground. If this is the moment in which you now find yourself, I invite you to take a moment and contemplate this story just a little bit more than you normally would.

What do you need to be more conscious of as you approach the completion of your project? What tasks require your attention? What help, if any, do you need? And if after reading this book, you perchance have newly committed to sharing your stories with the world, *what do you need to be most mindful of as you hop down from your branch, only five feet of the ground, to Mother Earth below?*

EXERCISE:
IT IS TIME TO TELL YOUR STORY

"A story is a way to say something that can be said no other way."

—Flannery O'Connor

Since you have made it this far in the book, I'm assuming you have some appreciation for the power of storytelling. I am also assuming you have enjoyed at least some of my stories. But that is not why I wrote this book. I wrote it because I want you and millions of other people around the world to share their stories with each other. Now that you have gotten this far, you are ready to take your next step towards the frontlines of storytelling. It's simple. All you need to do is fill in the blanks below. Once you do, you will have all the raw material you need to begin crafting your first story. Ready?

1. **Identify A Story You Want To Tell:** This can be a memorable experience from your own life or a story you have heard from someone else.

2. **Give Your Story a Catchy Title:** The act of naming your story gives it roots and increases the odds of it flowering. Now it's time to give your story a name that has some mojo to it.

3. **Know the Moral Of Your Story:** What is the message of your story – the key point you want to communicate?

4. **Describe How You Want Your Story To Make People Feel:** Every story is told to have impact. And that impact begins with *feeling*. How do you want people to feel after listening to your story?

5. **Tune Into Your Hero:** Every story has a protagonist – a hero or heroine who goes on a journey and overcomes obstacles. Who is the hero of your story? How can you make this person believable, intriguing, and likeable?

6. **Flesh Out the Setting:** All stories take place *somewhere*. Where does *your* story take place? And how, using just

a few images or details, can you help your listeners see this place in their mind's eye?

7. **Clarify Your Plot:** A story is a narrative, an account of something that *happens*. What happens in your story? What are three or four key plot points? Remember, you are not writing a 300-page novel. You are telling a brief story.

8. **Include a Compelling Obstacle:** If your story doesn't have an obstacle, it is not a story. Maybe it's an anecdote or a joke, but it is not a story. What is the danger/difficulty the hero of your story needs to overcome?

9. **Be Clear About Your Ending:** Amateur storytellers tend to ramble at the end of their stories. They don't know when to stop – or how. Oops! Not good. How does your story end? And while we're at it, how does your story begin?

10. **Explore the Key Message of Your Story:** Sometimes, after telling a story, a door opens and listeners will linger at the threshold, wanting to explore it further. What question might you ask, at the end of your story, to encourage your listeners to dig in a bit deeper with you?

PART TWO
The Field Guide

"The moment one gives close attention to anything, even a blade of grass, it becomes a mysterious, awesome, indescribably magnificent world in itself."

—Henry Miller

ON SEEING CLEARLY

"It's not what you look at that matters. It's what you see."
—Henry David Thoreau

Once upon a time there was a powerful, wise, and benevolent king who knew his time was coming to an end. Wanting to ensure that his kingdom continued to thrive after his death, he called his three sons to his side.

"Blood of my blood," he began, "I know my loyal subjects are expecting me to pass my crown on to my firstborn, which is perfectly understandable. But, I do not want my legacy ruled by assumptions, and so I am inviting the three of you to enter into a contest to determine whom the next king will be. I have designed the contest not to test your strength because I *already* know you are strong. Nor have I designed it to test your loyalty. I already know that, too. I have designed the contest to test your ability to see that which is not immediately apparent, since *seeing clearly* will be one of the most important skills you will need to rule wisely."

And with that he asked his grand vizier to escort the three boys down several long hallways and through a hidden doorway none of them had ever seen before.

"Wait here," he said. "Your father will arrive soon enough to explain the rules."

One hour passed. Then another. And another still. Then, with no fanfare, the king appeared, trailed by his courtiers, physicians, and his queen. Silently, he approached his sons and bowed.

"Flesh of my flesh," he began, pointing to a large wooden door before him. "In a moment, I will enter this room and stand in the middle of it. I will bring nothing with me, only my love for you and my curiosity. Then, one by one, each of you will have your turn. Three times I will perform this experiment. The door will open and beginning with my firstborn, you will enter, when it is your turn. Your task is a simple one – to tell me what you see in the room. That's it. But you will only have a brief amount of time to accomplish this task. If you take too long, you will be disqualified. Do you understand?"

And with that, the grand vizier turned the boys around so their backs were to the door. Then he grabbed the hand of the eldest son, walked him to the door, opened it, and spoke one word: "Enter." The boy walked in. The room was completely dark.

"Well," asked the king, "what do you see, my son?"

"Nothing, father. There is nothing here, but you."

"Thank you, my son. Well said. Now turn around and when the door opens, exit quickly."

Now it was the middle son's turn. The grand vizier approached, took him by the hand, walked him to the door, opened it and spoke one word: "Enter."

The boy walked in, the room still completely dark.

"Well, asked the king," what do you see, my boy?"

"Nothing, father," he said. "There is nothing here but you. And, of course, me, too."

"Thank you, my son. Well said. A most important distinction you have made. Now turn around and when the door opens, exit quickly."

Now it was the youngest son's turn. Again, the grand vizier approached, took him by the hand, walked him to the door, opened it and spoke one word.

Like his two brothers before him, the boy walked in. The room was still completely dark.

"Well," asked the king," what do you see, my youngest son?"

"Nothing, my father. I see nothing. And while I know I have only the briefest amount of time to reply, may I ask you a question?"

"Yes, my son, you may."

"In all your many years as king, what would you say is the most important thing you have learned?"

"Hmm…" replied the king. "An excellent question. Most astute. But my answer will only distract us from the task at hand. We have the next king to select now, don't we?"

But even as the king responded, the eyes of the youngest son began adjusting to the dark. Where just seconds ago, only blackness prevailed, now he began to see the faintest outline of things – a chair, a table next to it, and a candlestick.

"Oh father," said the son, "thank you for your sage counsel. You are indeed, a man of great wisdom. But before I take my leave, please allow me to tell you what I see: a chair, a table next to it, and a candlestick."

The king took a long, slow breath. Then he exhaled even more slowly. "Well done, my son, well done. You see clearly. And because you do, you shall inherit my throne!"

FOR YOUR REFLECTION:

One contest. Three sons. Three different responses. The first son, the eldest, spoke the truth. He saw nothing and said so, noting only the obvious presence of the king. The second son also saw nothing, but had the clarity to acknowledge his own presence in the room. The third son, the youngest, was the only one who understood that seeing sometimes takes time and that first impressions aren't always accurate – so he bought himself the time he needed by asking the king a question.

And so it is with the wisdom inside us. It is not always immediately visible to us. Indeed, it is often hidden from sight. And *where* it is hidden, more often than not, is in our *stories*

– the faraway room within us in which the king abides. If we want to see what's there, we need to give it some time. We need to be curious, ask questions, and allow our eyes to adjust, even if, at first glance, it seems as if nothing is there.

This is what Part Two of *Storytelling for the Revolution* is all about, a way for you to see what may be invisible to you now, the stories within you that are begging to be told. This Field Guide will help you discover the wisdom hidden in those stories and everything you need to know (and do) to tell them in the most meaningful way possible. Like the grand vizier and the king, Part Two cuts to the chase with as few words as possible. Your time is valuable. And so is mine. And besides, there are hundreds, if not thousands, of people waiting to hear your stories, the ones you haven't yet told. So let's get on with it, shall we?

REVOLUTION AND REVELATION

"Modern storytellers are the descendants of an immense and ancient community of holy people, troubadours, bards, griots, cantadoras, cantors, traveling poets, bums, hags, and crazy people."

—Clarissa Pinkola Estes

We, as a human species, are standing at a crossroads. Every one of us is facing a monumental choice – one that has a lot to do with the kind of lives we want to lead and the future of our planet. Heroes in all stories are faced with a similar choice. Do they take the high road or the low? Do they accept help from a stranger or go it alone? Do they face the beast head on or sneak out the back? That's what makes stories so interesting. The intrigue. The unknown. The conflicts navigated by the protagonist and how he/she deals with the inevitable obstacles that head their ugly rear along the way.

One choice we all have, as teller of tales, is the choice between *revolution* and *revelation*, two words that sound alike, but conjure up entirely different images in the mind.

Let's start with "revolution" – one of the words in the title of this book. Why is *revolution* a concept that storytellers need to be mindful of? Because every great story is a revolution, both in the sense of revolving around a core theme and being an uprising – a conscious taking on of an old way of being that needs to be overthrown, enabling the hero or heroine to be saved from the burden of whatever it is that has kept him or her down.

Bottom line, a storyteller is a kind of revolutionary, taking on whatever systems or structures are no longer working. Being a revolutionary can be an exciting path – energizing, absorbing, and purposeful. But pushing back against an existing order is only part of the story. It's easy to fight against "the wrong," but it takes an entirely different mindset to *live* "the right." This is precisely why a lot of revolutionaries who end up in power make terrible leaders. They don't necessarily have what it takes to sustain their breakthrough. And because they don't, they become ripe targets for the next revolution. And round and round it goes.

This brings us to revolution's twin, *revelation* – the disclosing of some kind of eternal wisdom – a universal blast of truth that can never be overthrown. Good storytellers are not just revolutionaries. They are *revelationaries*, too.

What do storytellers reveal? Two things: the access to *feeling* and the *re-cognition of untapped wisdom* – essentially what it means to be a conscious human being: curious, awake, aware, adaptive, resilient, creative, reflective, responsive, kind, compassionate, evolving, generous, grateful, and a whole lot of other words you can find in your nearest thesaurus.

That's why we tell fairy tales to our children. We want them to gain access to the wisdom inside them, which they will need to access as they mature. That's why we go to the movies, watch TV, or read books. We want access to wisdom – even if the path to this noble aspiration isn't always an easy one.

Simply put, you can't have one without the other. Revolution and revelation go hand in glove.

As a storyteller, your responsibility is to increase the odds of your listeners joining the journey with every ounce of their being – not as tourists, but as explorers of their own quest for insight, wisdom, love and yes – revelation.

ENTERING THE REALM OF THE EVOCATIVE

"Story reveals meaning without committing the error of defining it."

—Hannah Arendt

A good story, like good perfume, is evocative. Listening to one calls forth a response that moves a person from one state of mind to another, not just for the moment, but for all time, because a story, well told, is long remembered. And what it is that moves inside us is less about the plot, characters, and moral, but the *space of discovery* that the story evokes.

Music is a perfect example. A good piece of music is composed at least as much of pauses as it is of notes. Indeed, it is the spaces in *between* the notes that evoke the feeling – a feeling that allows the listener to not only hear the piece, but also experience it.

Amateur composers tend to do too much. They clutter their compositions with themselves, making the music more about their own proficiency than the depth of what's possible to evoke in their listeners – a phenomenon that led jazz-great, Dizzy Gillespie, to confess, "It took me my entire life to learn what not to play."

The same holds true with story. Skillful storytellers don't tell too much. They don't clutter the tale with their telling. Instead, they provide just enough space for the listener to enter into the story and *participate*. That's the goal of any work of art – to create the potential for something meaningful to be explored.

Ultimately, the storyteller's task is a simple one: *to create a stage upon which the heart can dance* – what hearing a cello in the distance evokes at dusk or how you feel just before opening a love letter.

WHAT IS WISDOM? WHO IS WISE?

"The only true wisdom is in knowing you know nothing."

—Socrates

In the world today, there are 6,500 spoken languages, 4,200 religions, 196 countries, 31 kinds of government, 12 astrological signs, and 5 major branches of philosophy. But there is only one name for the people for whom all this diversity is happening – and that is "homo sapiens."

"Homo sapiens," the scientific name for our species, originates from the Latin "homo" (human being) and "sapiens" (wise). The name of our race, simply put, translates as "the wise ones." It is *wisdom*, or at least the capacity for wisdom, that all human beings share in common, above and beyond our much-heralded opposable thumb.

OK. Good. Fine. But what the heck is wisdom, anyway?

To begin with, let's take a look at what it is not. It is not theoretical knowledge. It is not intellect. Nor is it a collection of philosophical insights. Wisdom is something else – *truth in action*, "the ability to think, discern, and act – born from knowledge and experience – that enables a person to be of the greatest service to others, often in situations where there is no obvious solution." In short, wisdom implies a possession of awareness that, when applied to a given situation, especially one that is not easily resolved, ensures the best possible outcome.

A classic example is known as the "Judgment of Solomon." As the story goes, two women came to Solomon to resolve a quarrel to determine the true mother of a baby. When Solomon suggested they should divide the child in two with a sword, one of the women immediately blurted out that she would rather give up the child than see it killed. Solomon declared *that* woman, the one who showed instant care and compassion, to be the true mother and gave the baby to her. One point for Solomon.

A modern-day example of wisdom can be found in the musical, *Fiddler on the Roof*.

Two men, in the town square, are having an argument over a recent business transaction. The buyer claims that the "horse" he bought from the seller was actually a "mule," while the seller loudly proclaims that the animal was, in fact, a horse. Back and forth they argue, each making their case, when finally they see Tevyev, the town milkman, standing nearby. Calling him over, the buyer makes a case for why the animal he bought was not a horse, but actually a mule. Tevye listens, strokes his beard, and declares, *"You're right!"* The seller, aghast at Tevyev's judgment, proceeds to make an equally solid case for why the animal was a horse, and not a mule. Tevyev listens, strokes his beard, and again declares, *"You're right."* Meanwhile, a neutral observer, who had been closely watching the exchange, steps forward, turns to Tevyev and blurts: "Wait a minute! How can he (pointing to the buyer) and he (pointing to the seller) both be right?" Tevyev listens, strokes his beard, and declares *"You're right!"* Then he starts dancing.

I realize, of course, that if you are a lawyer or a breeder of horses or mules, Tevyev's answer may not satisfy you, but at another level, his brilliant answer addresses a much bigger issue – the tendency we all have to think we're right.

If you study the literature of the world's spiritual traditions, you will find that story predominates as the preferred medium for communicating wisdom – collections of parables, allegories, legends, and tales embedded with the distillation of a particular tradition's highest truths – non-didactic teachings that spark insight, awareness, and the kind of meaning that can easily be remembered.

For example, to make the point I am now making, I could have chosen to summarize the 293,000,000 articles I found when Googling "wisdom" or I could have told you two simple stories – the *Solomon* story and the *Fiddler on the Roof* story. The first approach would have taken me an insane amount of time and have bored you to death. The second approach, the story approach, cut to the chase in less than two minutes and can be easily remembered. No philosophy. No mental gymnastics. No existential debates.

Who is the wisest person you know? And what about the way this person operates in the world has convinced you that he or she is, indeed, wise?

WHY PEOPLE TELL STORIES

"It has been said that next to hunger and thirst, our most basic human need is for storytelling."

—Kahlil Gibran

Some people go to Mexico to lay on the beach. Some go to get a good deal. Others go to escape the law. Different strokes for different folks. It's the same with storytelling. The motivation varies from person to person and sometimes varies for the same person on different days. Here are the top seven reasons why people tell stories:

1. **To Discover What They Already Know:** I don't know what your nationality is. Neither do I know your religion, philosophy, or IQ. But there is one thing I do know: You are a member of a species that some have called "the crown of creation." A quick glance at the evening news will likely reveal otherwise, of course, but if you dig deeper, you cannot help but notice that our species has learned a thing

or two along the way. And not just how to use our opposable thumbs, but other, less measurable accomplishments. Like how to be compassionate, how to be grateful, and how to be of service to others – all aspects of what it means to be self-aware or, as Socrates put it 2,500 years ago, what it means to "know thyself."

All of us have had at least one know-thyself moment along the line. For some people, this moment may have been triggered by the birth of a child. For some, it was a near-death experience. For others, maybe it was being on the receiving end of a stranger's random act of kindness. For most of us, these moments are fleeting. Like dreams, they quickly fade from memory. But out of sight, does not necessarily mean out of mind. *Invisible* is not the same thing as *non-existent*. Our moments of wisdom may be simply hidden from view. They hide, more often than not, in our stories – the life experiences we've had that, once told, give shape to insight, feeling, and lessons learned.

Tuning into our stories allows us to reverse engineer what we know – to decipher the hidden wisdom of our lives. Just like the atom contains protons, neutrons, and electrons, our stories also contain *essence* – the invisible distillate of our life's experiences. The microscope we need to observe this distillate? Our own curiosity, much in the way an archeologist is compelled to dig beneath the surface of things. But curiosity is only half of what's needed. The other half? *Speaking* our experiences out loud – *telling our stories*, even before we think our stories are ready to be told. Because, more often than not, it is in the *telling* of our stories that light is shed on our wisdom.

2. **To Capture Attention:** This just in: The attention span of the average human being is one second less than the attention span of a goldfish. According to Canadian researchers, the average goldfish can concentrate for nine seconds. The average homo sapien? Eight. The reasons for our distractibility are many, but the biggest can be attributed to our increasingly digitalized lifestyle. There's simply too much coming at us these days to stay focused on anything for very long. And so, we look for shortcuts. We tweet. We text. We check our Facebook newsfeed. Knowing that you, dear reader, have only an eight-second attention span, I am going to cut to the chase and give you one more reason to tell your stories. *They capture attention!* They help your audience unplug from their mental chatter and focus. Assuming you have something of value to say, it can only happen if people are listening. And a story, well-told, is the simplest, fastest, most effective way to do that.

3. **To Connect With Other People:** What do most people on a first date do besides wonder why the person they are talking to looks older than their match.com photo? *They tell stories.* That's how people get to know each other quickly. Because in the telling of our stories, the other person gets a chance to see who we are beneath the surface – our values, our interests, and what moves us. Yes, on a first date, we might dress up. We might put on cologne or perfume. We might tell a joke or two. But the most effective way to get closer to

another person is to share our stories. Boundaries dissolve. Rapport is established. Doors open up.

4. **To Elevate The Conversation:** 90% of the news you are exposed to is bad news – updates on death, destruction, war, corruption, fires, floods, and terrorism. That's why journalists like to say, "If it bleeds, it leads." Human beings have what sociologists call a "negativity bias" – a phenomenon that can be traced to our amygdala, the survivalist part of our brain that is our built-in danger detector. If you hear something rustling in the leaves, your amygdala interprets it as danger, a possible tiger ready to pounce, instead of the gentle rustling of the wind. Get enough people focused on the negative and you have the state of the world today, everyone primed to expect the worst. But it doesn't have to be that way. And that's where storytelling comes in, your chance to change the narrative, to tell stories that uplift, awaken, and inspire. I'm not suggesting that you ignore the bad news. I'm suggesting that you consider your options – you have a choice about what to talk about.

5. **To Transmit Tacit Knowledge:** Years ago, when people wanted to learn a trade they would apprentice themselves to a Master, someone who deeply understood how to accomplish a particular outcome in the most effective way possible. Indeed, in Europe, the guild system was set up to facilitate this kind of knowledge transfer. Those days are gone. Few people, in the 21st century, have the time or humility to become apprentices anymore. Now we Google what we want to learn. Or maybe download a video. And while there are definitely things that can be learned this

way, the deep transmission of "tacit knowledge" (i.e. the hard-to-communicate-essence of a particular realm of understanding) doesn't naturally happen that way.

Still, there exists, in our world today, a classic technique of knowledge transfer that goes largely untapped. And that is storytelling. When a story is told, assuming it is the right story, told in a compelling way, at the right time – it has the potential to get to the heart of the matter quickly. And by so doing, it has the potential to spark great insight, awareness, and meaning. Indeed, since the beginning of time, storytelling has been one of the most effective ways that the world's wisdom traditions have passed on their knowledge to the next generation.

6. **To Increase Listening In The World:** Here's the paradox: No matter how powerful a story might be, it will have no impact unless there is someone listening. And listening, these days, is in short supply. Most people, who strike the appearance of listening, aren't. Instead, they are impatiently waiting for their turn to speak. I call this "conversational endurance." And it seems to be getting worse with each passing tweet. Is there any way to reverse this phenomenon? Yes, there is. And, if you are up for the paradox of it all, *storytelling* is the way to go. Because when you tell a story, assuming you tell it in a compelling way, the people on the receiving end get to practice listening. They get to experience what it is like *not* to interrupt. They get to experience what it is like not to counter with a fact, question, or objection. In short, they get to *practice the art of listening*. My hope? The more people that listen to your stories, the more their "listening

muscle" will be exercised and the more able they will be to listen to other people in non-storytelling situations.

7. **To Honor Your Elders:** My father was a storyteller – not professionally, but in his everyday life. Other than yelling and stomping around the house, storytelling was his preferred means of communication. My response, as an all-knowing teenager, was to ignore, deflect, or judge his storytelling. "Not again." I would think to myself. "Jesus, I've heard this story a thousand times before."

Heard? Yes. But listened to? No. More often than not, I interpreted my father's storytelling as either a bogus way to hog the conversation or a feeble attempt to teach me something I already knew. And while I was, even as a young boy, very much into learning, I wasn't into being taught. Years passed. It wasn't until I was 45 that I understood the game I was playing. Addicted as I was to shooting the messenger, I was missing out on the message – one that was hiding in my father's stories.

Methinks my little story-resisting routine with my father is not all that uncommon. It's a phenomenon that plays out everywhere – not just from child to parent, but from generation to generation. Driven by our adolescent need to individuate, even the most conscious of human beings has a tendency to ignore the elders in their life, dismissing them as "old-fashioned," "irrelevant" or just not "cool enough." This just in: Not true. The stories of our parents, their parents, and the generations who preceded them are absolutely relevant. Indeed, they are part of our lineage and the collective unconscious of planet Earth, having, embedded within them, great meaning. The indigenous people of the world know this, big time. And always have. It is how the wisdom of their cultures have survived, one beautiful story at a time.

So, the next time you see an "old" person, realize they are not just old, but are a potential elder – an influential person of your tribe or community infused with the wisdom that comes from experience, even if they are not officially designated as a sage. They may not have the same politics, philosophy, or spiritual path as you, but they have something even more important and that is the potential to be a catalyst of wisdom. Forget about the package for a moment. Forget about your judgments and your previous relationship with them. Just listen. Honor your elders. They have a gift for you and the gift is wrapped in story. All you have to do is open it.

HOW TO DISCOVER YOUR STORIES

"The most important question to ask is: 'What myth am I living?'"

– Carl Jung

Astronomers, in 1996, attempted a very interesting experiment. They pointed the most powerful telescope in the world, the Hubble space telescope, into a part of the sky that seemed to be empty, a patch of the universe assumed to be devoid of even a single planet or star. This experiment was a risky one, since time on the Hubble telescope was expensive and in high demand. Indeed, there were many respected scientists, at the time, who questioned whether "looking at nothing" was a wise use of time and resources. Nevertheless, the experiment proceeded.

When the experiment ended, 10 days later, and the images were processed, more than 3,000 galaxies had been detected – each galaxy containing hundreds of billions of stars.

Eight years later, in 2004, astronomers decided to perform the experiment again, this time pointing the Hubble telescope towards a totally different patch of sky – a section of the universe also assumed to be empty. At the end of this second experiment, 10,000 new galaxies were discovered, each one also containing billions of stars.

As a writer and storyteller, I have asked many people to tell me their stories – moments of truth in their life or just something interesting that happened to them that week. Not infrequently, the people I ask look at me with a blank stare, explaining that they really don't have any stories to share – that not all that much has happened to them in their lives.

Metaphorically speaking, I am directing their attention to a patch of their own night sky and what I hear back from them is that there is nothing there.

As a long-time researcher of the storytelling phenomena, I know their conclusion is not even remotely close to true. Each and everyone of us, no matter what our life experiences have been, contain a universe of stories within us: memorable happenings... moments of truth... rites of passages... unforgettable encounters... lessons learned... cool stuff... and a whole bunch of personally meaningful experiences. And yet, when we are asked to identify our stories, we often draw a blank – kind of like those skeptical astronomers who assumed there was nothing to see in deep space.

You have stories inside you. You do. Of course, you have stories! If your life depended on it, you could identify at least ten of them in the next few minutes. And if I offered you a thousand dollars, you could come up with a whole lot more.

Why then, are so many of us blind to our stories? Why do so many of us insist there is nothing much to see or say?

Three reasons: First, most of us assume that a story needs to be earth-shattering in order for someone to be interested, and because most of our stories are not earth-shattering, we forget them quickly or never notice them in the first place. Second, we don't take the time. Remember, the astronomers who pointed the Hubble Telescope into deep space did it for 10 days, not 10 minutes. And third, most people don't know where to look or how to look. The "technology" we use to detect and unpack our own stories is not very sophisticated.

Consider this: If you look into the night sky with only your own two eyes, the most you are going to see, on a good night, is 3,000 stars. There is no way in the world you will be able to detect that the universe is actually 47 billion light years wide with an estimated 100 trillion galaxies, each galaxy containing hundreds of billions stars.

You and I, my friend, are also universes. We are. Inside of each of us are seven billion billion billion atoms. That's a one with 27 zeros after it. And while we might not have seven billion billion billion stories inside us, we certainly have more than a few, each one capable of lighting up the night sky. And not just for ourselves. Also for the fortunate ones who get a chance to listen to them.

If you want to discover your stories, you will need to change the way you look for them. And, of course, before you begin looking, just like our Hubble Telescope astronomer friends, you will need to get *curious*.

HOW TO TELL A GOOD STORY

"If a story is not about the hearer he or she will not listen. A great lasting story is about everyone or it will not last. The strange and foreign is not interesting – only the deeply personal and familiar."

—John Steinbeck

There are only three things you need to understand in order to tell a good story: 1) your purpose; 2) your story's structure, and 3) how to sustain people's interest.

1. PURPOSE: If you are moved to tell a story, begin by asking why. *Why do you want to tell that particular story?* What is your purpose, your aim, your intention? The clearer you are about the results you want, the more effective your story will be. If your purpose is merely to break the ice, then a joke or anecdote will suffice. Indeed, for some people, storytelling is just *shtick* – a light-hearted gimmick, honed over time, that serves to loosen people up. On the other hand, if your purpose is deeper, you will need a different kind of mindset, preparation, and delivery. In this case, you're not looking for *shtick*, but something that *sticks* – something that will awaken, inspire, and enlighten. Being in touch with your purpose is the storyteller's tuning fork – the simplest way to ensure the tale you tell has impact.

2. STORY STRUCTURE: If you want to build a house, it's useful to have blueprints. It's also useful to know what the basic elements are that give a house *structural integrity*. Like the foundation, for example. Like the walls. Like the roof, windows, and doors. The same holds true for storytelling. A good story, like a house, has *structure* to it – fundamental elements that allow it to stand and provide shelter from the storm. Once you understand what these elements are and how to put them in place, you're on your way. Let's take a look at five of them:

- **Character:** Every story needs a hero or a heroine. And this character needs to be likeable, vulnerable, or intriguing in some way – someone on a mission who the audience can root for. Creating a hero is not as difficult as it may seem, especially in the oral tradition. Since you will not be writing a 300-page novel, you won't need to concern yourself with the kind of nuanced structural issues that drive most novelists insane. All you need to do is give your hero a bit of personality. For example, note the difference between the following two opening lines of a story: "Once upon a time there was a salesman" vs. "Once upon a time there was a dyslexic salesmen who had just returned from a tour of duty in Afghanistan." The second description takes just a few seconds longer, but provides the listener with a picture far more likely to engage an audience. Think of it this way: You are a movie producer and the movie you are producing is playing inside the mind of your audience. If your audience can visualize your hero or heroine and feel connected to him or her in some way, you have succeeded.

Who is the hero of your story? What about this character is intriguing?

• **Setting:** Luke Skywalker did not have his adventure in a shopping mall. He had it on the Falcon, a spaceship from the future. And also in the Star Wars bar. And on some mythical planets. Big difference. Since you and your listeners exist in time and space, you will also need to place your story in a *setting*. Wherever it is, you want to give your audience enough details to be able to visualize that setting and be transported there. Know this: if you do not pay enough attention to setting, it will be *upsetting* to your audience. Their ability to go along with you for the ride will be greatly compromised.

Where does your story take place? What makes this place interesting?

• **Plot:** Technically speaking, the following is a story: "I woke up. I took my clothes to the dry cleaner at rush hour. I returned home." Yup. That's a story. Is it a meaningful story? No. A memorable one? No. One you are likely to tell your friends? No. And one of the reasons why is because the plot is lame. An interesting plot is one that includes intrigue, mystery, and surprise. The audience doesn't know what's coming next and are on the edge of their seats. Our little dry cleaner story doesn't exactly meet this criteria, does it? Since spoken stories are short, you won't need too many plot points, but you will need some – a set of events that follow a logical progression. If you don't know what your plot points are, you don't have a story. You have something else. Maybe a "show and tell." Maybe a lecture. Maybe a sermon. But not a story.

What are the three key plot points to your story? Where does your story twist and turn?

• **Obstacles:** Do you know how many versions of "Little Red Riding Hood" there are in the world? 119! Almost every culture on planet Earth has its own version of this classic tale. And one of the reasons *why* is because of the Big Bad Wolf – the archetypal obstacle in the way of the damsel in distress. A story without an obstacle is like a bagel without a hole. Something is missing. Indeed, it's the nemesis/boogeyman/monster that provides the drama that makes a story captivating. What would Perseus have been without the Medusa? Luke without Darth Vader? Cinderella without her evil stepsisters? In a word, *boring*. One of the most common reasons why storytellers disappoint is because there are no obstacles in their stories or their obstacles are not well-developed.

Who or what is the obstacle in your story? How can you give it more dimension?

• **Resolution:** Resolution is the a happy ending of a story – or, if not happy, then at least an ending – how the drama of your story resolves, what the protagonist learned that will serve him or her (and, hopefully, your listeners) for the rest of their lives. In a fairy tale, the resolution is the moral. In a joke, it's the punch line. In a Sufi, Zen, or Hasidic Tale, it's the spiritual teaching. If your story does not have a resolution, it's not done. Like an unfinished symphony, there is no final chord. The clearer you are about your story's resolution, the more powerful your story will be. The *delivery* of the message, of course, can be done poorly or done well. Done poorly, your audience ends up confused, having to struggle too hard to decipher what your story means and how they can apply its message to their lives. On the flip side, you can be absolutely crystal clear about your story's message, but beat your audience over the head with it, showing little respect for their intelligence or discovery process. Somewhere in between these two poles is the sweet spot you're going for.

What is the message of the story you want to tell? How does it resolve?

3. SUSTAINING INTEREST: Some storytellers are so talented they could recite the phone book and keep you captivated. Others are so untalented they could make your favorite story sound like a late night reading of *The Federalist Papers*. The difference is in the *telling* – not so much the *what*, but the *how*. Good storytellers know how to engage an audience. Bad storytellers don't. Here's what good storytellers do:

- **They Hook Your Attention Quickly:** Bill Gates once began a talk on malaria by opening a jar of mosquitos and releasing them into the room. Not particularly known for being a good storyteller, Bill's opening gambit did the trick. It got him the attention he needed to make his point and take everyone along for the ride. You won't need to release a jar of mosquitos every time you tell a story, but you will need a skillful way to begin. While there is no right way to do this, there are some time-tested strategies that work. You might, for example, preface your story with a sneak preview of it, as in "I'm just about to tell you a story about the time I came within three seconds of drowning." Or, you could begin with a bit of audience participation: "Raise your hand if you have almost drowned." Or, you might begin with a compelling first sentence. "I wasn't always a highly paid keynote speaker. Just four years ago I was on death row." The key? Finding a hook, the way to cut through the noise inside the mind of your audience and engage them quickly.

- **They Are Authentic:** A good storyteller knows how to elicit trust from their audience. In just a matter of seconds, they can get you to not only like them, but also believe them. If there was a campfire with marshmallows, you can see yourself sitting around it. Something in you can tell they are not playing a role, not performing, not posing. They've got nothing to sell, no hidden agenda, no wool to pull over your eyes. All they want to do is tell you a story. Garrison Keillor is a master of this. When you listen to him, you know, in a heartbeat, he is authentic. And though he may have told this same story for the past 30 years, not once does it feel rehearsed or memorized. And *why* it doesn't is because the illustrious Mr. Keillor knows his story so well he can, like a really good jazz musician, be in the moment with it – and with you, the listener. Like an old pair of jeans, it fits everybody.

• **They Use Their Whole Body:**   Most people assume that the storyteller's main instrument of delivery is their *mouth*. After all, that's where the words originate, right? Not true. The storyteller's main instrument is their entire body. Mimes use no words, but tell amazing stories. Their movements, facial expressions, and hands speak volumes. Indeed, a skilled mime can often tell a better story, *without words*, than most of us can tell *with* words. Psychologists tell us that 55% of all communication is body language, 38% is tone of voice, and only 7% the words. Good storytellers know this intuitively and use every medium at their disposal to deliver their message. Here's the bottom line: when you are telling a story, you are, for the moment, a one-man or one-woman show. You are on stage and stage craft matters – how you move, where you move, when you move, the pacing and volume of your voice, the accents you affect, when you pause, when you don't, the look on your face, and the way you use your hands. All of it matters.

• **They Paint Pictures and Make Movies:** Which of the following sentences are most interesting to you: "The boy walked into the room" or "The boy, with his father's army pistol in his twitching left hand," walked into the room? The first sentence is six words and takes three seconds to speak. The second sentence is 16 words and takes seven seconds. But the second sentence paints a very different picture. This is precisely what good storytellers do. They paint pictures. They make movies. They provide colorful details – all of which move you from one state of mind to another. Good storytellers don't just want you to *hear* what they say, they want you to *see* what they say. Because when you see what they say, you will be better able to feel what they say. And the more you *feel* what they say, the more their story will stick.

• **They Evoke:** Good stories are like perfume. They evoke feelings, change mood, and lower resistances. Half art, half science, storytelling has the power to move people from one state of mind to another and, in the process, transport listeners to another world. Actually, storytellers who have mastered the *art of evoking* are far more than storytellers. They are also wizards, magicians, enchanters, and shape shifters. The word "evoke" originated from the French "evoquer" and the Latin "vox." Its meaning? To "call out, rouse, or summon." That's what a storyteller does. And guess what? It has a lot to do with *voice*.

- **They Simplify:** Good storytellers are like chemists or, on a good day, *alchemists*. In the underground lab of their imagination, they are busy mixing this, that, and the other thing in the hope of distilling their message down to essence – the kind of essence that will end up infusing their stories with the distillate of their secret sauce. Not-so-good storytellers are like flea market addicts, forever cluttering their storytelling with unnecessary trinkets. As a result, their stories are overly complicated. The thread gets lost and so does the needle. Deathly afraid that their stories will not be enough to engage their audience's attention, they compensate by loading them up with unnecessary plot points, details, and characters – sometimes even going so far as to shoehorn in other stories that don't belong. Less is more.

- **They Connect With Their Audience:** Whether it's one person you are speaking to or 10,000, if you want your story to have impact you will need to connect with your audience. This is simpler to accomplish than you might imagine, assuming you are not afraid of people or thinking you are inferior or superior to the people in the room. If you really want to connect with your audience, the first thing you will need to do is some research in order to understand their needs, mindset, and aspirations. Secondly, you will need to make eye contact. The eyes, it is said, are window to the soul. And it's true. Taking the time to look someone in the eye makes things quickly personal. It humanizes you and the people you are communicating to. In reality, you are not really talking to "an audience." You are talking to *people*. And, more specifically, you are talking to *individuals*. The more attention you pay to connecting with the individuals in your audience, the more your story will connect to the whole.

• **They Architect Their Story:** Builders of houses usually work from a blueprint, an architect's rendering of what the finished house will look like. World travelers usually have an itinerary in place before they take off for parts unknown. Party planners have a sense of the flow of the events they produce. Good storytellers also have a plan. There is an inherent logic to their stories – an architecture to ensure their telling has structural integrity. This appreciation of form frees the storyteller from having to make everything up on the spot, adrift in a sea of infinite possibilities. If you know what the key mileposts are in your story, you won't need notes or a PowerPoint show to keep yourself on track. You will know your way forward.

• **They Improvise:** Big rock stars make a lot of money playing big venues. But if you ask big rock stars where they would prefer to play, a lot of them will tell you "small clubs." Why? Because a different kind of music happens for them in small clubs. They are reading not only their charts and other members of the band, but also the body language of their fans. Just like the monitors installed on stage provide the feedback they need to be on top of their game, so does the feedback they get from their audience.

Musicians are not just playing *for* their audience, they are playing *with* their audience – their improvisations often a function of the subtle cues they receive from the people in the room. Storytelling works the same way. Though the storyteller may have rehearsed a story 20 times before, it is the reaction of their audience that enables the storyteller to adapt and adjust the telling of their tale. All of this, of course, only happens if the storyteller is tuned into their audience, not just performing a set piece.

• **They Enjoy the Experience of Telling Their Story:** In my entire life, I don't think I have ever listened to a depressed storyteller. Droll? Yes. Laid back? Yes. Subtle? Yes. But not depressed. Maybe they were depressed 10 minutes *before* they began or 10 minutes *after*, but not *during*. The feeling storytellers radiate is almost always upbeat and engaging – like they cannot wait to tell you something interesting. Audiences pick up on this enthusiasm and the quality of their listening is enhanced. If you, as a storyteller, are not enjoying your experience of telling your tales, there is very little chance your listeners will.

HOW TO RAISE THE ODDS THAT PEOPLE WILL LISTEN

"Most of the successful people I know, do more listening than talking."
—Bernard Baruch

When small children speak their first words, the reaction of their parents is fairly predictable. It begins with lavish praise, high fives, hugs all around, and the ritual calling of Grandma and Grandpa. Everyone is thrilled. The baby has spoken! But the first time that same child *listens*? No response at all. No lavish praise. No calls to the grandparents. Indeed, it's a rare set of parents who even *notice* when their child listens for the first time.

As a species, we more highly value *speaking* than *listening*. Everyone needs the ability to express, to makes one's case, and being *heard* is a primary need. Listening, on the other hand, is not – suitable, perhaps, for people with nothing much to say or nothing better to do than be on the receiving end of someone else's monologue.

In high school, you will find debate clubs, but no listening clubs. On the political circuit, "stump speeches" rule. It is the rare politician who goes out on a listening tour. Bottom line, the people who make the strongest case win. And the people who are listening? They don't win. They may be *hearing*, but hearing is different than listening. Mostly, "conversational endurance" occurs – people who strike the appearance of listening, but are simply impatiently waiting to have their turn to speak.

You know the expression "If a tree falls in a forest and there's no one around to hear, did it really make a sound?" The same holds true with storytelling. If a story is told, but no one is listening, is it really a story? I don't think so. Words may be uttered and words may be heard, but the actual story falls on deaf ears.

There is no storytelling without story listening. But story listening is in very short supply these days. Well, then, what's an aspiring storyteller to do given this non-listening state of affairs? In a phrase: *everything possible to ensure that the stories they tell are actually listened to.* And while this is easier said than done, it is possible. What follows are seven ways for you to increase the odds of your stories being listened to:

1. **Choose the Time and Place Wisely:** Instead of blurting out your story on the fly, be attentive to the readiness of your audience to listen. If the people you want to tell your story to are on the run or distracted, do not begin. Not only will your story fall on deaf ears, but

you are likely to end up feeling diminished. Choose a different time and place. And, if you forget this simple guideline and notice your audience is not listening, cease and desist! Say something like, "It seems like this might not be the best time for me to share my story. Might there be another time and place that might be better?"

2. **Get Permission:** Instead of reflexively launching into your story (which is likely to be perceived by the "other" as an unwanted invasion of their time and space), ask for permission. "Mind if I share a two-minute story that very much relates to what we're talking about?" Once the listener gives you permission, the odds of their listening increase dramatically.

3. **Preview Your Story:** Before launching into your tale, provide the listener with some context, a preview of what will come. "This little story happened to me five years ago on a plane, " you might say. Or "what I'm just about to share with you changed my life in just three minutes." Or, "I think the little story I'm about to tell you is the simplest way to think about the topic we are wrestling with."

4. **Stay Connected to Your Audience:** Sometimes storytellers, intoxicated with their own stories, end up in "air guitar solo riff" territory. Enamored by the sound of their own voice or the fact that they have any kind of audience at all, they lose connection with time and space. Fun for them, perhaps, but not for the listener. Stay connected to your audience! Tune in!

Make eye contact. Notice their body language. Adapt and adjust your storytelling to the subtle cues and feedback you are being given.

5. **Go Beyond the Words:** Communication experts tell us that there are three main elements to any communication: Body language, voice dynamics, and the words being spoken. Of these three elements, body language is the most important, it accounts for 55% of the impact of what's being said. Voice dynamics is the second most important aspect of communication and accounts for 38% of the impact. The words themselves? Only 7%. So, if you want to increase the odds of people actually listening to your story, be mindful of your body language and voice dynamics.

HOW TO IDENTIFY THE SEED OF YOUR STORIES

"The world is not made of atoms. It is made of stories."

—Muriel Ruykeser

No one knows, for sure, exactly how many species of fruit there are on planet Earth, but with 7,000 species of apples, alone, it's fair to say there are hundreds of thousands, most of which you have never tasted. Inside of each of them is not only a sweetness, but a seed – or many seeds – nature's way of ensuring the proliferation of that particular form of nourishment. The seeds come in all shapes and sizes, but no matter what shape or size they may be, if you want to get to the seed, you will need to get past the rind, or in some cases, the shell.

And so it is with story. Stories also have seeds, the embryonic life force contained within them. But getting to the seeds of a story is not always easy. To begin with, the rind of a story, especially our own story, can sometimes be difficult to penetrate. Secondly, our stories often contain more than a single seed. The first one may be easy to find, but the second or the third may not. And finally, the person trying to locate the seeds doesn't always have the motivation, tools, or tenacity to get past the rind. And so, the story just sits there like a piece of fruit in a bowl. It may have color. It may have shape. It may have texture, too, but it's essence remains unexplored.

In modern-day parlance, the seed of a story is called the "moral"– the key point, lesson, or message. In most fairy tales, the moral is relatively easy to identify, which is why we tell them to children. "The Three Little Pigs"? Hard work and dedication is often the difference between life and death. "Little Red Riding Hood"? Obey your parents and don't talk to strangers. "Cinderella"? Go beyond obstacles and seek your highest dreams.

But your stories and my stories don't always reveal their essence as tidily as fairy tales. The messages contained within them are often hidden from view. Effort is required to get to the core, but it is an effort well worth it. Why? Because contained within the seeds of our stories is the distilled essence of our deepest insights, knowledge, and wisdom. Our stories are a kind of secret code. Encrypted within them are clues to the mystery and meaning of our lives, a kind of hieroglyphics of the soul. Yes, the meaning of the stories we tell is sometimes obvious and requires no deciphering. But other times, inner archeology is needed – committed digging, poking, and prodding into the hidden chambers within.

If this kind of self-inquiry interests you, it is my pleasure to offer you some digging tools – tools, in the form of questions, to help you make your way past the rind.

These questions can be asked of two different kinds of audience. The first audience is you. After writing or telling a story, you can ask yourself one of more of the following questions to help you get to the core meaning of the story. The second audience is everyone else. But remember, if someone tells you one of their stories, you will first need to get their permission before asking your questions. Some people, after telling a story, especially a personal one, are not comfortable being asked questions about it. To them, it may feel like an invasion of privacy or a poorly timed analytical exercise. So before asking any of the following questions to the storytellers in your life, make sure you get their permission. If they say, YES, you're on your way. If they say NO, thank them for sharing and move on.

Ready to dig?

1. If there was a moral to the story, what would it be?

2. How would you describe this story in 25 words or less?

3. How would you explain this story to a five-year old?

4. What are three things you learned about the hero or heroine of the story?

5. What do you find most fascinating about the story? Surprising? Revealing?

6. How has the story given you pause or changed your outlook on life?

7. If there was a part of the story you wanted more of, what would it be?

8. If this story was going to be made into a movie, what would it be called?

9. What elements of the story require more reflection on your part?

10. In what ways can you apply the message of this story to your own life?

GOOD STORYTELLING IS ALL ABOUT TIMING

"Sometimes I arrive just when God's ready to have someone click the shutter."

—Ansel Adams

"Timing is everything" goes the old saw. Indeed it's what distinguishes a good joke from a bad joke, a yummy meal from indigestion, and a memorable performance of Beethoven's Fifth from a forgettable one. It's not enough to have something of value to give people. Equally important is *how* that something of value is given. Serve the cheesecake *before* the salmon and you screw up the meal. Pause too long before your punch line and the joke bombs. Bang your drum three beats *after* the violin solo begins and get ready for the wrath of the conductor. The same holds true for storytelling. No matter how profound your story may be or how good of a storyteller you are, if you tell it at the wrong time, it's worse than if you haven't told it at all.

Why is this phenomenon so common? Too many storytellers are overly focused on what they want to say rather than why. Bottom line, they are out of touch with their audience – whether it's an audience of one or a thousand. As Abraham Maslow put it, "If all you have is a hammer, everything looks like a nail."

Too many storytellers are wielding their stories like hammers. And so, the pounding begins.

At the grossest level, timing-challenged storytellers are like telemarketers calling you at dinnertime. *Their* need to sell you something has little to do with *your* need. Their need rules the day – their need to be heard, or seen, or perceived as wise. Rather than delivering a meaningful communication to you, their storytelling becomes nothing more than an interruption of your life, a foisting of their own need to speak with little relationship to your need to listen, a verbal invasion of privacy. Maybe this is why so few people are willing to listen to stories these days. Too many times they've been hammered by others trotting out their pet stories like infomercials.

Is there a way out of this madness? Yes, there is. And the quickest, most reliable way to begin is to realize that storytelling is, first and foremost, *an act of service*. What follows are five simple guidelines to help ensure that the stories you tell are actually of service to others:

1. **Read the room.** Or, if there is only one person in the room, read the person. What clues do you get from their body language and facial expressions? Do you sense their readiness to listen to your story? Or do they need to tell one of their own – a chance for you to listen.

2. **Tune into the theme that is front and center.** Does the story you want to tell relate to this theme? Will the telling of it shed more light on this theme or will it distract people from the topic at hand?

3. **Pause. Allow space.** Let there be silence. Rather than reflexively telling your story upon recognizing you have a story to tell, wait a bit, even if it's just a few seconds. Take a breath. Those few extra seconds of pausing are sacred. They create more space for whatever will best serve the moment. Maybe someone in the audience will enter that space. Or maybe it's actually time for your story to be told, but not because you have rushed into the space, hair on fire.

4. **Create a bridge from what's being said to your story.** Instead of dropping your story on people like leaflets from a plane, create a segue that sets some context for what's to follow. Build a bridge, not a wall. For example, you might say something like, "That reminds me of a story – a sweet little tale likely to shed light on the topic we've been exploring."

5. **Be aware of how much you have already spoken.** If you've been center stage for a while, back off a bit. Give someone else a chance. You may have a great story to tell, but if the people in the room are starting to feel like you are taking up too much space, it's time for a breather.

WHY PEOPLE DON'T TELL THEIR STORIES

"The most courageous act is to think for yourself. Aloud."

—Coco Chanel

I'm sure you've heard the expression, "Suppose they gave a war and nobody came?" The same question holds true for the *storytelling revolution*. I can flap my mouth about the power of personal storytelling until the cows come home, but unless you and a critical mass of others step up, nothing much will happen. This is a volunteer army I'm talking about, a self-appointed crew of people willing to make their way to the frontlines and tell it like it is. Are there obstacles on this storytelling battlefield? Of course there are. But the biggest ones are *invisible* – old thoughts, assumptions, and beliefs that stop us from speaking up. Here are the ten most common.

1. My Stories Are Not Interesting Enough.

This is the biggie, the mother of all obstacles – the belief that you are not courageous or important enough to speak up, that your stories are mundane, insignificant, and meaningless. Nothing could be further from the truth. You are a human being, the "crown of creation." You already have a ton of experiences worth sharing. If you don't think your stories are interesting, it's probably because you haven't probed them deeply enough. In other words, if your story was a box of Crackerjacks, you haven't found the prize yet, or what William Blake once described as "eternity in a grain of sand." Bottom line, *everything becomes interesting the moment you become interested.* The stories you tell don't need to be earth shattering. They don't need to be cosmic. And you don't need to be a spokesperson to speak. All you need to be is a human being who wants to elevate the conversation.

2. No One Will Care About My Story. No One Will Listen.

Well, it is certainly possible that no one will care about your stories. And it is certainly possible that no one will listen. Your assumption about this, however, most likely comes from your past experience and, if you buy into this belief, it will become a self-fulfilling prophecy. Maybe, from time to time, you've made efforts to tell your stories and have had little success in getting people to pay attention. But just because it's been that way in the past, doesn't mean that's the way it's going to be in the future. Just because your last relationship ended poorly, doesn't mean your next one will. The same thing holds true for storytelling. If you want to increase the odds of people listening to your stories, honor the following guidelines:

- Make sure *you* care about your story. The more you care, the more others will.

- Practice telling it and get feedback from friends.

- Be sure to choose a time to tell it when people are most available to listen.

- Be animated in the telling of your story.

- Before launching into your story, set some context and get permission.

3. I Am Not a Good Storyteller.

OK. Here's the deal: *You are a way better storyteller than you think you are.* Hey, you grew up on fairy tales, watched TV, movies, and read books – all of which were made of stories. Indeed, 65% of your conversations, explain sociologists, are composed of stories. It's the DNA of how we communicate. Psychologists refer to this ability as an "unconscious competency" – the ability to do something without being aware we are doing it. Like breathing, or complaining, or riding a bike. One of the reasons you think you're not a good storyteller is because you compare yourself to other storytellers. Like Garrison Keillor, perhaps. Or your grandfather. Or your favorite TED speaker. Cease and desist! It's a waste of time. The storytelling revolution I'm asking you to participate in takes place on the *frontlines of your own life*, often with an audience of only one. But if you keep telling yourself you're not a good storyteller, you silence yourself. And silence is not what's needed now. What's needed is millions of people stepping forward to share what moves them. We can't wait for Sundays or someone "in a position of power" to shape the narrative. Look where that's gotten us. We need you and your friends to come out of the closet and let it rip.

4. I Don't Want To Be the Center of Attention.

And why might that be? Usually, because you don't like feeling self-conscious. Or maybe because you think people will think you are "full of yourself," "hogging the show," or otherwise being a prima donna. Fuggedabout it! While it may seem as if storytellers are the center of attention, the reality is this: the listener is the center of attention. Or, more accurately, the *meaning* of the story is the center of attention. The storyteller is just a catalyst, a facilitator of a moment of insight. Is an actor, on stage, the center of attention? For a brief moment, yes, but only to capture the attention of the audience so each person can feel something and take that something with them when they leave the theater. Each audience member then potentially becomes the center of attention in his or her own life. Of course, there are always people who want to be the center of attention at every opportunity: egomaniacs, narcissists, and anyone looking for approval. They care less about what people glean from the story than being remembered as the person who told the story. *But that's not you.* You are about speaking authentically and sparking moments of insight and understanding in others (and all without proselytizing, evangelizing, or trying to convince anyone of anything). Right?

5. It Will Be Too Stressful for Me.

Public speaking is a bigger fear for most people than the fear of death. You imagine yourself on stage with strangers frowning at you or checking their email under the table. Of course that would be stressful. But guess what? I'm not asking you to stand on stage. All I'm asking you to do is share your stories in the informal flow of your life. One-on-one, with your best friend, is fine. The storytelling revolution I'm inviting you to participate in is happening wherever you are. It's no big deal. There will be no marketing campaign, no slogans, and no dues to pay. And, if all else fails, remember the words of Mark Twain: *"If you speak the truth, you never have to remember anything."* Capiche? To tell your stories, you don't need to affect an English accent or look longingly into the distance. All you need to do is tell your story. Here's as simple as it gets: There's a person (you) with a goal and an obstacle to overcome. Then there's some kind of resolution. That's it. All I'm asking you to do, when the time is right, is share a meaningful story from your own life, a surprise moment, an unexpected victory, a lesson learned.

Hint: Speaking is not stressful. What's stressful is focusing on what people think about you as you speak.

6. I Am a Private Person. My Stories Are Not Intended for the Public.

Of course your stories are your own. They are no one's business until you *choose* to make it their business. Indeed, there are some indigenous tribes living in remote forests that believe that if someone takes their photo, they will also take their soul. This is sometimes how we feel when telling a story – that the person who has heard our story will now have power over us. This is especially true if you are identified with your story – an experience you may consider to be sacred. Telling one of those stories to a disinterested or judgmental audience will put you in the "pearls before swine" zone. That being said, you have two choices. You can choose not to tell stories about your life that are "out of bounds." Or, you can see yourself as a catalyst for change – that somehow, your life experiences, told in story form, may be of benefit to others. That's what Woody Allen does in his films. He puts his neurosis on the silver screen and takes one for the team. He gives shape to the collective psyche so the less adventurous people in the audience can get in touch with aspects of their own life that may be hidden. This takes courage, since some members of the audience may become so uncomfortable with what they see that they shoot the messenger. C'est le vie. If you truly want to be on the frontlines of the storytelling revolution, you will need to come out of your closet and let it rip.

7. I Will Be Judged.

Here's my simple answer: *Yes, you will be judged. So what?* First of all, you are already being judged almost all the time, including by the people closest to you. It comes with the territory of being human. You could, of course, choose to isolate yourself, armed only with your favorite mobile device and some ice cream, but even then people are going to judge you. *"Your Facebook posts are too long." "Your texts have too many typos." "You wait too long to respond to my emails."* What you need to remember is this: storytelling is not about you. Not only are you not the center of the universe, you are not even the center of your own story, even when logic dictates that you are. You may be a character in it – even the hero or heroine – but the real center of the stories you tell is the meaning other people derive from it – the learning or the insight they will be able to apply to their own life.

8. I Have Trust Issues.

See #7. Having "trust issues" is simply another way of saying you think people are going to judge you. You've been hurt before by others. Or ignored. Or misunderstood, blamed, abused, dissed, diminished, ridiculed, mocked, or disempowered. Yup. Welcome to the club. If you let trust issues have their way, forget about becoming part of the storytelling revolution. You'll be holed up in your house waiting for your next lifetime. Remember, my asking you to join the storytelling revolution is not the same thing as asking you to go on CNN as the spokesperson for the storytelling revolution. All it means is you are willing to share your stories with at least one other person from time to time.

9. People Will Change My Stories When They Share Them with Others.

Certainly possible, but so what? Songwriters, whose songs are covered by other singers, always run the risk of *their* songs being stylized until they're barely recognizable. What began as their song will be interpreted in countless ways by others. It will morph. It will change. A folk song may become a blues song. A blues song may become a rock song. This is not a bad thing. It may, in fact, increase the shelf life of the song. So let people change your stories. Remember this is really not about you anyway. You are just the messenger. This is about the meaning people will make of your story and how they will apply the essence of it to their own lives. Your storytelling is just a way to get the party started.

10. My Story Isn't Ready Yet To Share.

Ah… welcome to the fabulous world of paradox. The thought that your story isn't ready to share can be true and untrue at the same time. Indeed, it is the *tension* between these two polarities that most commonly leads to inaction. On one hand, it is may be true that your story isn't ready for primetime. You may be in the process of incubating it, refining it, or hatching the "story egg," so to speak. If you tell your story too early, you may end up trotting out a half-baked message that will fall with a thud. Here's another side of the storytelling coin for you to consider: Sometimes, the assumption that "my story isn't ready to share" is simply a function of *perfectionism* – the same reason why you don't try anything new. You tell yourself you don't have enough information, or enough degrees, or haven't done enough research. Be mindful of this tendency. Sometimes, the only way your story will be ready to share is to tell it. Or what Tom Peters meant when he said, "Ready, fire, aim!" This is the same reason why many Broadway plays start off in Peoria. If your story's not read to share, practice sharing it!

HOW TO READ AN AUDIENCE

*"Do not dwell in the past. Do not dream of the future.
Concentrate the mind on the present moment."*

—Buddha

A strologers read stars. Meteorologists read weather. Palm readers read palms. And storytellers? *They read people.* At least good storytellers do. No matter how many times they have told a story, the way they tell it depends on the subtle cues they pick up from their audience. Eyes and ears open to the signals their listeners are sending, good storytellers adapt and adjust their delivery accordingly.

Simply put, storytelling is a lot like dancing. It is not a static art form, not a canned speech, not the repetition of memorized words. Rather, it is an in-the-moment expression designed to move people. And while it is true that, just like dancing, there are steps, patterns, and structures to learn and practice, the difference between a good story and a great story is often a function of the storyteller's ability to improvise.

What is the responsive storyteller paying attention to in order to make the kind of subtle adjustments needed to ensure their story sticks? In a phrase, *the in-the-moment feedback communicated by their listeners* – the cues and signals their audience exhibit, *consciously or unconsciously, to convey or hide their true feelings*. Whether it's one person across a kitchen table or a thousand people in an auditorium. The more the storyteller can pick up on this feedback and *adapt*, the more successful their storytelling will be.

What kind of feedback are we talking about? Two kinds: *facial expressions* and *body language* – peoples' responsiveness (or lack thereof) to what they are seeing, hearing, and feeling. Like head nods, for example. Like smiles and frowns. Like the way a person looks or doesn't look or where they look. Like the way a person leans forward or backward in their chair or folds their arms or rolls their eyes or grunts or sneaks a glance at their cell phone. All of it matters. All of it. All of it communicates its own story to the storyteller. The more storytellers can sense these cues, the more they will be able to adjust the dynamics of their delivery: How fast to talk or how slow. Whether to pause or not and when. How dramatic to make their voice. When to move and when to stand still and when to elaborate on a detail that has caught the audience's fancy and when to move on.

If you, as a storyteller, are nervous, self-absorbed, seeking approval, or impatient for the whole thing to end, it will be difficult to catch the signals coming your way.

You won't truly be with your audience. While you may be physically inhabiting the same space, metaphysically you will be somewhere else. Will real communication have taken place? Doubtful. Words may have been spoken. Characters may have been introduced. Points may have been made. But the real story will have gone untold.

HOW TO USE STORIES TO COMMUNICATE BIG IDEAS

"Think of a story as a mnemonic device for complex ideas."

— Annette Simmons

A priest, a penguin, and a newspaper reporter walk into a bar. The penguin orders a shot of Red Eye. The priest starts juggling three flaming chain saws. The newspaper reporter turns to the bartender, smiles and says: "I know there's a story here somewhere."

And yes, there is. *There are stories everywhere.*

Almost everyone in business these days, at least the people responsible for selling big ideas, know that the difference between success and failure often depends on what kind of story is told and how well. Content may be king. But it is story that built the kingdom. Or as Steve Jobs put it, "The most powerful person in the world is the storyteller."

The question isn't whether or not storytelling works. It does. It's worked for thousands of years. The question is *how do you tell an effective story*, one that not only informs and entertains, but also gets results – the kind of results that opens minds, influences behavior, and is remembered.

And this is precisely where the plot thickens. Because most people don't think they know how to tell a good story. At least, that's the story they keep telling themselves – that they don't have the chops or experience to tell a good story. Spoiler alert! Not true.

You already know how to tell a story. You do. You've been telling stories ever since you were a child. In fact, you tell stories many times a day. On the job. Off the job. Hanging out with friends. Wherever. Story is in your DNA. Indeed, neuroscientists like to say that the human brain is "wired for story." It's how we make sense of our lives. It's our communication default position. We are storytelling animals. And the more we practice, the better we get.

The simplest explanation of what a story is? A narrative – an account of what happened or what might happen. That account, of course, can be utterly boring or it can be utterly captivating – what every movie you've ever seen or novel you've ever read has tried to accomplish. To capture your attention. To deliver a meaningful message. And to influence what you think, feel, and do.

For the moment, think of storytelling as a big, yummy pot of soup. It smells good. It looks good. And it tastes good. But at first glance, you can't tell what the ingredients are or the spices.

Do you really need to know every single ingredient if you're being served a bowl of soup from a reliable source? Probably not. But if you're making the soup, you most definitely do. So let's sit down with our penguin, priest, and newspaper reporter for a few minutes and see if we can demystify what this whole mumbo jumbo story thing is all about.

First things first: If you want your story to pack a wallop, you've got to know your audience. If they're allergic to eggplant, don't put eggplant in the soup. If they're vegetarian, lose the chicken. Know your endgame – what it is you're trying to communicate – what you want your audience to think, feel, or do differently after listening to you. Whatever message you want to leave them with, be able to boil it down to ten words or less.

Years ago, this would have been known as your "elevator speech." These days, if you can't deliver your message upon *entering* an elevator, you're screwed. Think about it. When Steve Jobs launched the iPod, he cut to the chase by distilling his message down to just five words: "1,000 songs in your pocket." Technobabble? No. Overwhelming factoids and data? No. One clean soundbyte surrounded by a compelling beginning, middle, and end. When you think about the story you want to tell, be sure you can distill it down to a memorable meme – what screenwriters do when they pitch their idea to a movie studio.

Just like the iPod has a shape, so does a story – the beginning, the middle, and the end, as I've said before, but

I'm saying again! I want you to remember the importance of structure. It's the spine of your intended result.

The beginning is where you set things up – the place where you hook the attention of your audience, the place where you set the scene and introduce your hero or heroine, hopefully likable. Then you introduce the Big Bad Wolf – the obstacle, the conflict that begets the drama. Get the picture? Someone or something exists and that someone or something wants to move towards an inspired goal, but his/her/its path is blocked. Time for nail biting and some popcorn. Hooray for adversity! Without it, there is no story. No *Star Wars*. No *Rocky*. No "Three Little Pigs."

And the broth of the story soup you are concocting? What might that be? Passion! *Your* passion. Your passion for the message you're communicating and your passion for the act of storytelling itself. No passion, no power. No passion, no presence. No passion, no purpose. It's that simple.

Bottom line, story is all about "emotional transportation" – the journey you take people on from *here to there*, from *known to unknown*, from *no can do* to *what's the next step*?

No matter how logical, linear, or analytical your audience might be, unless you can speak to their heart, you will never win their mind. Yes, of course, if you are making a business presentation, you will need to spice up your story with the fruits of your research, but only enough to soothe the savage beast of the left brain. Data is the spice. It is not the main ingredient. If your audience isn't *feeling* what you're saying, it doesn't matter how many statistics you throw their way. It's Little Red Riding

Hood on her way to Grandma's house that we care about, not her shoe size or SAT scores.

Other things to be mindful of? Keep your stories short. Speak in the language of the people, not the technologists. No one wants to hear an epic poem. What you're trying to do by telling a story is create an opening to drive the Mack truck of possibility through and maybe pick up a few hitchhikers along the way. You are building a bridge, not a shopping mall.

Lose the complicated backstory. "The world doesn't want to hear about your labor pains, they want to see the baby," said baseball great, Johnny Sain. Your team may have put a lot of effort into a project. Months of work. That's great. That's nice. Show us the baby!

And please don't read from your PowerPoint slides. Not only is that boring, it's rude. There's no way you can build rapport and read the room if you are staring at a screen. If you want your audience to look into the future, you've got to look into their eyes, not one boring slide after another.

And when you want to crank things up, consider asking a compelling question or two. Then pause and listen to the response. The more you listen, the more your audience will listen. Know that a good story is also a good performance. So, unhinge yourself from the dead zone, the spot on the floor to which you have nailed both of your feet. Move around the room. Vary the lengths of your sentences and the volume of your voice. Gesture. Make facial expressions. Speak to one specific person at a time, not the generic audience. But above all, *trust yourself.* If you don't trust yourself, no one else will.

Of course, you can only trust yourself, if you are prepared. So practice your ass off. Know your talking points. Write out a script. Understand the flow of what you want to say, the key milestones along the way and whatever anecdotes and facts you want to include. Then distill the whole thing down to few main points on note cards. Then throw your note cards away. Or, if you absolutely need to hold onto your note cards, glance at them only occasionally. Otherwise, they will become a kind of 3x5 PowerPoint show in your hand, yet another slow leak in the bucket of your storytelling brilliance.

Remember, there is no formula for telling a good story, only guidelines. And there is no one right way to tell a story. There are thousands. Maybe millions or billions, each one according to the personality of the teller. Your job is not to tell a story like Steve Jobs, Garrison Keillor, or Winston Churchill. Your job is tell a story like you! And while it is perfectly fine to read books on storytelling, study TED videos, and attend instructional workshops, in the end, all you need to know is this: You are sitting around the tribal fire with the elders. They want to hear from you. You've been on a big adventure for days, weeks, or even months. You've got important news to share with them, memorable experiences to convey. The survival of the tribe depends it. You're not trying to get promoted. You're not worried about being cast out of the tribe. The only thing that matters is telling your story in a way that informs, inspires, and enlightens. End of story.

THE DARK SIDE OF STORYTELLING

"I suppose the most revolutionary act one can engage in is to tell the truth."

—Howard Zinn

Storytelling is like water. It can quench your thirst or it can drown you. Or maybe storytelling is like a knife. It can slice open an orange or it can poke your eye out. Simply put, storytelling is a two-sided coin. One side gives life, the other takes. One side is authentic, the other is counterfeit. And this is, precisely, where the plot thickens, because story, the most effective communication tool human beings have at their disposal, has been used in both ways since the beginning of time. Yes, some people use it to heal, inspire, and enlighten. But others use it to deceive, control, and manipulate. This book has been written for the first group, the group, I imagine, you identify with. But no matter how much you identify with the first group, there's always a chance you might, without knowing it, find your way, subconsciously, into the second group, especially during times of stress, fear, or anger.

Let's take a brief tour of the dark side by looking, first, at advertising. Technically speaking, advertising is nothing more than the practice of calling public attention to a product or service. Is that an inherently bad thing? No, it isn't. Unless, of course, the way in which our attention is being called is ruled by manipulation, control, or deception. Advertisers, for the most part, are motivated by one driving force – to get you to buy what they're selling, whether or not what they're selling is actually something you need. They need to sell it, but you may not need to buy it – that is, until your choices have been shaped by your psychological responses to the ads they keep sending your way. Do you know what story advertisers communicated in the 1950s? That smoking was actually good for your health. Tell that to my mother, who died of emphysema, at 83, after six decades of smoking unfiltered Chesterfields.

Political spin-doctors also walk on the dark side of storytelling. Along with thousands of others watching the news, they listen to the words of the President or the politician du jour, but before the viewing audience has had the time to form their own opinions, the spin-doctors do the forming for them. And how they do that is by quickly telling a new story about the story the viewing audience just heard. They interpret what's just been said in whatever way is most likely to sway opinion. The Big Bad Wolf wasn't really all that bad, you see, he was just sleep-deprived or maybe his eyesight was failing. Donald Trump wasn't lying, he was just presenting "alternative facts."

Trial lawyers are masters of this dark art, especially when they deliver their closing arguments. Armed with exactly the same information that has been presented to the jury for weeks, the prosecuting attorney and the defense attorney tell completely different stories. They pick and choose from the facts that most support the conclusion they want others to believe and they string them together in a way that makes their conclusions seem like fact, when they may not be. And the masters of the trade distill the new story down to as few words as possible. "If the glove don't fit, you gotta acquit" was the eight-word story Johnny Cochrane told the jury in defense of O.J. Simpson – and we all know how that turned out.

Perhaps the grossest example of storytelling gone south is "revisionist history" – what happens when people, with an ulterior motive, attempt to rewrite the past to suit their own needs. The history of early America, for example, is primarily a narrative crafted by white colonialists who specialized in killing Native Americans and stealing their land. "Westward ho!" was the plotline. "The pioneering spirit" was the leading man's motivation. And the back-story? "The early settlers quest for religious freedom." Murder? Rape? Plunder? Barely mentioned. Do you think the Apache, Cherokee, and Oneida are telling the early settlers' version of American history around the tribal fire? No way. Their story, the real story of what happened, goes unheard in public schools. "Those who tell the story, rule the world," explain the Hopis from their underfunded reservation in Oklahoma.

None of my family died in The Holocaust, but I have many friends whose family did. Six million Jews died in concentration camps. But the taletellers of the Holocaust denial movement communicate a very different story these days. They claim, with great passion and "proof," that Nazi Germany's final solution was aimed only at deporting Jews and had nothing to do with exterminating them – that gas chambers and concentration camps never existed. And they figure if they tell that story enough times to enough people, popular opinion will change. And it has. There are now thousands of people around world who actually believe The Holocaust was a hoax.

Closer to home, the dark side of storytelling (or at least the grey side of storytelling) plays out in just about every marriage in the world. Here's how it works: A conversation begins between husband and wife, one that quickly polarizes both partners. He sees it one way and she sees it another. Buttons get pushed. Old wounds surface. He said/she said rules the day. Which quickly leads to the husband and the wife crafting their own stories about the contentious topic at hand. Each spouse blurts their story to the other, but because feelings are running so high, neither story is heard, and, even if it is, it is not believed. Which leads, of course, to the husband and wife each seeking out their own friends to tell their stories to – the sole purpose being to get validation. The stories make sense. They are told with great passion. Heads nod. Comforting gestures are made. The wife's friends conclude the husband is a jerk and the husband's friends conclude the wife is a bitch. And on and on it goes. 50% of the time this saga ends up in divorce court, an extraordinary stage where lawyers, far better tale tellers than their embroiled clients, get paid big bucks to concoct the most convincing stories possible for the judge. Does anyone live happily ever after? Rarely. But a lot of money exchanges hands. And a lot of children will have sad stories to tell, years later, to their own children.

In the end, it all comes down to this: we have two choices. One choice is to be of service to our fellow human beings – to uplift, inspire, and awaken. The other choice is to serve our selves, ruled only by the need for attention, approval, validation, power, control, money, fame, ratings, or our lifelong addiction to hearing ourselves talk.

What choice will you make?

HOW TO GO BEYOND STAGE FRIGHT

"I learned that courage was not the absence of fear, but the triumph over it."
—Nelson Mandela

Research into human psychology has revealed that the average person is more afraid of public speaking than they are of death. Indeed, it appears as if most people would rather be motionless in their own coffin than deliver the eulogy. "Stage fright" would be the operational term for this phenomenon. Many storytellers experience it whenever they stand up in front of an audience – a mindset that is not conducive to memorable communication. In a moment or two, I'm going to lay out ten guidelines to help you get over your stage fright. But for now, let's take a look at what this whole fear thing is about.

Fear is a feeling induced by the perception of danger or threat. This perception of danger or threat results in a change in metabolic functioning that leads to a change in behavior –

a response that results in four different fear-based reactions: fighting, fleeing, freezing, or flocking. While fear is a feeling that is not all that enjoyable to experience, it is not, necessarily, a bad thing. In fact, fear has a purpose – a primal purpose – to radically increase our chances of survival. Its roots, gnarled as they may be, go all the way back to the Stone Age. If a cave man or woman heard the roar of a lion nearby, it made perfect sense for them to enter into a fear state because fear triggered the kind of mindset that increased their chances of behaving in a way that ensured their survival. Their fear reaction triggered the release of chemicals in their body – adrenaline, cortisol, and glucose – all of which helped our ancestors make the kind of moves that helped them live another day.

Sometimes, however, people experience fear when there is no life-threatening danger. The rustling of leaves in the bushes outside your bedroom window doesn't necessarily mean a serial killer is preparing to attack you. Perhaps the sound you are hearing is due to a sudden gust of wind or maybe your neighbor's neurotic cat is obsessing about a mouse. To your amygdala (the part of your brain triggered by fear), it doesn't matter. It interprets the rustling of bushes as BIG DANGER and the next thing you know you are hiding in your room, running into the kitchen, looking for a knife, or calling 911.

What is going on in the mind of the public speaker when they mount the stage? Why the sweaty palms, butterflies, dry mouth, and, in some cases, the hope that the building will catch on fire?

In a word, fear. Is this reptilian-brained emotion justifiable? No. On the contrary, it's the result of an out-of-control, monkey-mind imagination – wild thoughts that conjure up danger when no danger exists.

What is the storyteller's most common fear? Being rejected. Because being rejected implies that they will be ostracized from the community. And while this fear may seem ridiculous to family and friends, it is well founded. You see, back in the day, the most effective way a community punished their members was to cast them out of the tribe. And when a person was cast out to "fend for themselves," their survival was very much at risk, what with all those lions and tigers just waiting to pounce.

And we carry this false equivalency deep within our psyche. No wonder public speakers get uptight. Just about to open their mouth (to speak, not scream), they imagine that what they have to say is going to be judged and they will be rejected, cast out of the community into the savannah, jungle, or forest of their own fevered mind. No wonder people would rather lay silent, in their own coffin, than give the eulogy. At least, in the coffin, they won't be forced to endure the slings and arrows of the people who have gathered to pay their last respects.

Is there a way out of this "wind-rustling-in-the-bushes-outside-your-bedroom-window" syndrome? Yes, there is. Actually, there's more than one and here they are – *The Idiot Savant's Guide to Speaking Your Truth in Front of a Group of People Without Breaking Out in Hives*:

1. **Remember Your Purpose:** The more clarity and commitment you have about the message you want to deliver, the less stress you will feel. Clarity rules!

2. **Acknowledge the Fear You're Feeling.** Okie dokie. You are afraid. Now ask yourself *what* you are afraid of and what will happen if the outcome you're afraid of comes to pass. Let's say it does. Now what? Are you going to die? Well, yes, eventually, but not on stage, tonight. It might feel like that to you, but the feeling is your survival instinct working overtime. As the psychotherapist Fritz Perls once said: "Awareness cures." Stay aware!

3. **Reframe Your Fear:** Once you get curious about your fear, you can use it as an opportunity to learn something about yourself. And the simplest way to do that is to ask yourself a question to get curious about. You get to decide what that question is. The question I like to ask myself when I get the heebie jeebies: "What's the worst thing that can happen?" Somehow, the simple act of asking that question diminishes my anxiety.

4. **Visualize Your Success:** In your mind's eye, see the impact you want to have on people. In other words, imagine your story/presentation is a smashing success. What are the people in the audience going to feel as a result? How will their lives be benefited? Bring it to mind. Feel it.

5. **Remember a Time When a Story You Told Went Well:** Feel what it felt like. You've told a story before, right? Maybe you told it to a friend. Maybe you told it

around a campfire. Maybe you told it at a meeting or conference. Bring that moment to mind. Connect with the feeling of it. Savor it.

6. **Realize That Fear Is Normal** and that everyone gets afraid, even the best speakers. Hey! You are not the only one ever to feel anxious when addressing a group of people. You are a human being! That's a good thing!

7. **Practice Your Story In Advance:** The more you practice, the more comfortable and confident you will be. Have a map of your story in your mind. Know where you are going with it. If you need to, jot down the three to five key points on a note card and glance at it before you go out on stage.

8. **Know How You Want To Begin and How You Want To End:** "The beginning," said Plato, "is the most important part of the work." And it's true for storytellers, as well. Know your opening line. Know your ending, too.

9. **Let Go of Trying To Be Perfect:** Public speaking is not about perfection. It's about authenticity. The people in your audience don't want to listen to a person giving a flawless speech. They want to listen to a real human talking about something they have passion for. That's you!

10. **Speak To the Individual, Not the Mythical Group:** There may be 10,000 people in your audience, but you are not talking to "them," you are talking to the individuals who make up that 10,000 – people just like you and me, people with issues and problems, people with hopes and dreams, people who would never, in a

million years, have the courage you have to get up on stage and speak. The best way to talk to these people is to make eye contact, one person at a time. And if, perchance, the person with whom you are making eye contact is frowning or in a bad mood, don't waste your time trying to convince or convert them. That's probably the way they are with their husband, wife, children, mother, father, and co-workers. Just move on to the next person until you find someone whose glance becomes an oasis for you.

HOW YOUR STORIES CAN BE AS CREATIVE AS POSSIBLE

"To live a creative life, we must lose our fear of being wrong."

—Joseph Chilton Pierce

OK. Here you are, almost at the end of the book. Congratulations. Now, by the grace of the storytelling gods, you should be primed to begin your process of preparing a story to tell. How can you do this in the most creative way possible?

1. **Identify what blocks your creativity:** When Michelangelo was asked how he made his iconic statue, "David," he explained, "I simply took away everything that wasn't." From his point of view, the statue was already in the stone. All he needed to do was remove what obscured it. *What is in your way of telling or writing your stories? What can you do, this week, to remove that clutter?*

2. **Immerse:** Creative people have a unique ability to dive in and stay with a project for long stretches of time. They don't just hit and run. Instead, they get absorbed. That's why Einstein once said, "It's not that I'm so smart. It's just that I stay with problems longer." *How can you make more time to dive into your storytelling project?*

3. **Reframe failure:** Creative people are less afraid of making mistakes than most people. They understand that many experiments are needed and that trial and error comes with the territory. When Thomas Edison was asked how it felt to fail 800 times before coming up with tungsten as the filament for the light bulb, his reply said it all, "Fail? I didn't fail once. I learned 800 times, what didn't work." *How can you create more storytelling experiments in your life?"*

4. **Go beyond your limiting assumptions:** Often, the suppositions we make at the beginning of a project are completely bogus – a strange concoction of our past experiences, false beliefs, and personal myths. Innovators have a knack for being less bound by limiting assumptions than most people. Their state of open-mindedness allows them to explore bold, new territory. *What is your biggest limiting assumption about being a storyteller? What can you do to go beyond it?*

5. **Stay inspired:** I know of very few depressed or despondent people who are consistently creative. And while it's true, that creative people can sometimes get depressed or despondent, they don't stay in that space for very long, realizing that a positive mindset is one of the keys to their

success. *What is the simplest way you can stay inspired as you proceed with your storytelling project?*

6. **Ask WHAT IF:** Asking powerful questions is a great way to enter into creative mindset. And of all the questions you can ask, asking "What if?" is the most powerful. *What if you weren't afraid to fail? What are three other "what if" questions you can ask yourself?*

7. **Make connections between seemingly disparate elements:** One of the qualities of a creative thinker is the ability to *synthesize* – to see new relationships between this, that, and the other thing. MTV, for example, is nothing more than a new connection between music and television. Drive-in banking? A new connection between cars and banks. *What new connections can you make between seemingly unrelated elements of your storytelling project? List all the elements of it, then look for intriguing new connections between them.*

8. **See through others' eyes:** One of the biggest obstacles to creativity is our odd habit of viewing everything through our *own* eyes/lenses/filters. Addicted to our habitual point of view, we develop a weird kind of tunnel vision. The simplest way to free your self from this constraint is to look at your storytelling project through the eyes of someone else. *How would Bernie Sanders proceed if he was in charge? Rosa Parks? Richard Branson? Lady Gaga? What clues about proceeding do you get from their approaches?*

9. **Pay attention to your subconscious mind:** Ideas come to us from two places: the conscious mind (i.e. brainstorming, thinking, planning) and the subconscious mind (i.e. dreaming, hunches, fantasizing). Most great ideas seem to

come to people from the subconscious mind, when they are taking a break from the routine and not trying so hard. *Where and when do your best ideas come to you? How can you honor these ideas more than you currently do?*

10. **Suspend logic and linearity:** Most of us are rational beings. Our default condition is logic and linearity. But there's another part of us, too – the free thinker, the dreamer, the one who likes to play with possibilities. How can you suspend your tendency to allow logic and linearity to dominate? *How can you play around with possibilities more than you usually do?*

11. **Trust your instincts, intuitions, and hunches:** Albert Einstein once said, "Not everything that counts can be counted; and not everything that can be counted, counts." Indeed, when he got stuck, he used to conduct what he called "thought experiments," a fancy name for daydreaming. Bottom line, he trusted his hunches more than most of us do. *What are your instincts and intuitions telling you about your emerging desire to tell more stories?*

12. **Entertain the fantastic:** Gary Kasparov, the former Soviet Union Grand Chess Master, had the ability to strategize 26 moves ahead. But when, in 1989, he was asked what enabled him to beat Big Blue, IBM's mainframe computer, in a two game chess match, he attributed his success to "the ability to fantasize." Einstein, too, was a big advocate of fantasizing and is famous for having said "the ability to fantasize has meant more to me than my ability to absorb positive knowledge." *How can you make more time, in your life, for blue-sky thinking?*

13. **Collaborate:** Some people assume that creativity is the result of a lone-wolf genius inhabiting an ivory tower and returning to the marketplace with a brilliant breakthrough. And while this sometimes happens, it is mostly a myth. Often, creativity is sparked by being in relationship to other people – jamming, brainstorming, and playing around with new ideas. *How can you increase the amount of creative collaboration in your life? Who, specifically, can you invite to be one of your collaborators?*

14. **Have more fun:** This just in! "Aha" and "haha" are very much related. In the *aha* moment, the person with the insight ends up *surprised* about a given outcome. He or she is dislocated from their common assumptions, i.e. Archimedes in the bathtub. The *haha* moment is similar. Indeed, the reason why most of us laugh is because our expectations get disrupted. Creativity and humor are joined at the hip. Get too serious and you diminish the odds of creativity flourishing. *In what ways can you infuse your creative process with more playfulness and humor?*

15. **Look for happy accidents:** Do you know what penicillin, Post-It Notes, and Velcro have in common? They were all the results of accidents in the lab. None of them were the result of a brainstorming session or a strategic plan. But instead of being dismissed as mistakes, the innovators associated with these discoveries, got curious. They played around with these unanticipated occurrences until they discovered their commercial value. Indeed, research indicates that 75% of all product and service breakthroughs are the results of serendipity, surprise, and

happy accidents. *What curious insights have you stumbled upon recently that the logical part of you may have dismissed as inconsequential?*

16. **Change environments:** Sometimes, the simplest way to spark creativity is to change environments. Socrates knew this. That's why he invented his "Peripatetic School of Education" – a way to get his students to "walk the talk." This is why so many of us get our best ideas during or after exercising. *Where can you go, to refresh and renew yourself whenever you are feeling stuck?*

17. **Be comfortable with ambiguity:** Creating something new is not a function of a sequential process. It often requires lots of time spent not knowing or being confused. Ambiguity comes with the territory. If you are not mindful of this phenomenon, you will likely grab onto the first seeming "right idea" just to settle yourself down. This is not a good idea. *In what ways can you give yourself more permission to be uncomfortable as you proceed with your storytelling project?*

18. **Acknowledge your progress:** Creating something new is often frustrating. Results don't always come quickly. Consequently, aspiring innovators tend to get discouraged and enter into a cranky mindset. Inspiration, optimism, and positivity go out the window. The simplest way to neutralize this phenomenon is to take a few minutes at the end of each day to acknowledge the progress you have made, no matter how small. Think about your emerging storytelling project. *What progress have you made on it today? This week?*

19. **Give and receive feedback:** Often, aspiring innovators are on the right track, but their addiction to being right gets in the way. What they need to do in order to open up their creativity is get feedback from people they trust. Unfortunately, this happens rarely. All too often, we interpret feedback as criticism, so we don't ask for it. *In what ways can you get more feedback about your storytelling telling project? Who can you ask today?*

20. **Honor your polarities:** People who want to be more creative would love there to be some kind of blueprint or map. Guess what? There isn't. And even if there was, it would include contradictory directions. That's because the act of being creative is often a contradictory process, which is why Niels Bohr, the Nobel-prize-winning physicist, once said: "Now that we have met with paradox, we have some hope of making progress." The creative process is not an either/or phenomenon. It's both. Which of the following polarities are familiar to you?

- Patience/Impatience
- Solitude/Collaboration
- Urgency/Relaxation
- Seriousness/Playfulness
- Divergence/Convergence

What other polarities do you experience in your creative process? What can you do to honor them more than you currently do?

HOW TO FACILITATE WISDOM CIRCLES

"There have been great societies that did not use the wheel, but there have been no societies that did not tell stories."

—Ursula K. LeGuin

If you are interested in sparking more storytelling in others, what follows is a simple way to begin. You do not need to be an experienced facilitator to do this, nor do you need to be a great storyteller. All you need is an appreciation for story, a love of people, and the willingness to stretch your wings. Facilitating wisdom circles is easy to do is because everyone *already* knows how to tell stories, even if they don't think they know how. Your job is simple: to create the container for storytelling to take shape. There is no one right way to do it. There are many. In time, you will find your way. The key is to be authentic, enjoy the process, and be open to learning from experience. So, here goes, ten guidelines to get you started:

1. **Create a compelling invitation.** Very few people have ever been invited to a Wisdom Circle (or whatever you end up calling it). Consequently, they have no idea what it is. Your job is to create an invitation that is clear and compelling.

2. **Ask people, at least one week before your gathering, to identify a story they want to tell at your gathering.** This story needs to be one they are passionate about and can be told in less than five minutes – a story, the meaning of which, they are willing to explore with others.

3. **Choose a conducive meeting space.** Wisdom Circles can happen anywhere. But wherever you have one, be sure the space is comfortable, private, and suitable for people to listen, focus, and feel at ease. A circle of chairs is usually a good way to set up the room.

4. **Keep it small.** While the size of the group is up to you, it is advisable to limit the group size to 12 or less. This creates a sense of intimacy and increases the odds that a sizable percentage of the group will get a chance to share their stories.

5. **Explain the purpose and the ground rules.** After people are seated, welcome everyone, introduce yourself, explain your role, and restate the purpose of the gathering (i.e. to share some of our "moment of truth" stories and learn from each other in a relaxed way). Be sure to let people know when the session will end and what the ground rules are:

   - Listen with respect

- Be fully present
- Participation is voluntary (nobody is required to tell a story)
- No cell phone usage
- No therapizing, criticizing, or preaching
- Maintain confidentiality (what's said in the room stays in the room)
- Allow you to facilitate

6. **YOU begin the storytelling.** Once the ground rules are communicated (and agreed on), you tell the first story to get things rolling. Keep your story to five minutes or less and be mindful not to be too theatrical or a "storyteller superhero" which will only intimidate the group and make it less likely for anyone else to step up and tell their story.

7. **Engage the group after your story is told.** When you finish telling your story, ask the group to respond to one or more of the following questions. Allow no more than ten minutes for this reflection, so you leave enough time for others to tell their stories. The goal here is to help the group unpack the seeds of wisdom embedded in their stories.

- What do you think the moral of my story is?
- What aspects of my story touched you the most?
- How would you describe this story to a 5-year-old?
- Can any of you relate to my story? If so, in what way?

- In what ways do the themes of my story relate to your life?

8. **Open up the storytelling process to the rest of the group.** After your story is told and the group has had a chance to respond, ask "Who would like to go next?" Remind everyone of the five-minute-or-less storytelling time limit and that it will be your job to facilitate the process of the group responding to the next story told.

9. **Continue the storytelling process.** After the second story is told and the group has interacted, open up the floor to the third story and the fourth and so on, but be mindful of the time and group energy. There is no need for everyone to tell a story, nor is there need to overload people with too many stories. If people are engaged and inspired to go beyond the agreed upon time limit, check in and ask if they want to extend the session for another few minutes.

10. **Establish closure.** Ending the session well is just as important as beginning it well. There is no one right way to do this, but here are some guidelines:

- Acknowledge everyone for their participation.

- Ask the group what they liked about the experience.

- If you've prepared a feedback sheet, invite people to fill it out.

- Invite people to stay after for informal schmoozing.

- If you've scheduled a second Wisdom Circle, let people know when and where it is, and invite them to help you get the word out.

- If you think participants would enjoy this book, or my previous one *Storytelling at Work*, have some available for purchase.

- Encourage everyone to continue telling their stories outside of the storytelling circle to keep the spirit of storytelling alive.

HOW TO OWN YOUR POWER AS A STORYTELLER

"In the midst of winter, I found there was, within me, an invincible summer."

—Albert Camus

Years ago, in a faraway land, there lived a sorcerer who was in a bad mood most of the time. One day, in an especially cranky frame of mind, he decided to work his dark magic in a particularly nefarious way. He cast a spell throughout the land that locked everybody's arms at the elbow. The first few days of this massively uncomfortable condition wreaked havoc through the land, especially at mealtime because people could no longer feed themselves. The only way anyone could get food into their mouths was to eat like animals, an option that was not a particularly popular one to this proud race of people. Indeed, mostly everyone chose to go hungry rather than eat like dogs. That is, until the second day of this mass affliction when one particularly bright young girl came up with a brilliant idea. "If it is no longer possible for us to feed ourselves," she announced, "then let us feed each other!" Bingo! Problem solved!

Know this, oh aspiring storyteller: the service you are about to perform is very similar to the service provided by the people whose arms were locked in place. Every story you tell will be food for your fellow man and woman – an offering infused with nutrients that will nourish, strengthen, and give life. The only thing required is that you extend yourself to others.

This is the revolution I am talking about, the going beyond the "every man for himself" syndrome to lend a hand to in the most life-affirming way possible – the simple effort to feed the ancient, universal hunger for insight, wisdom, and love that lives inside us all. And while there may be thousands of ways to do accomplish this noble goal, one of the simplest ways is to tell your stories.

You don't need to be a genius to do this. You don't need to be a hero, wizard, or orator. All you need to be is a human being. And guess what, you are!

ABOUT THE AUTHOR

Greetings. Mitch Ditkoff here. I wrote this book and another award-winning book on the same topic: *Storytelling at Work: How Moments of Truth on the Job Reveal the Real Business of Life*. Both books are available on Amazon and in my garage. Oh, I also wrote *Awake at the Wheel: Getting Your Big Ideas Rolling in an Uphill World* and a book of poetry, *Full Moon at Sunrise*. When I'm not writing books, I'm captaining the good ship, **Idea Champions**, an innovation consulting and training company based in Woodstock, New York and San Miguel de Allende, Mexico. My work is all about helping people wake up to who they really are and how they can best be of service to others. I hope, in some small way, I have accomplished that goal with this book.

My wife, Evelyne Pouget, is a peace artist and the Founder of OneVoice, an organization that helps teenagers become humanitarians. We have two amazing children: Jesse, 23, works in the tech industry in San Francisco. Emilia, 21, is a fourth-year student at Hampshire College in Amherst, Massachusetts.

If you want to get in touch with me, I'm just an email away: mitch@ideachampions.com.

LINKS

"If you tell the truth, you don't have to remember anything."

—Mark Twain

MY WEBSITES

- MitchDitkoff   mitchditkoff.com
- Idea Champions   ideachampions.com
- Brainstorm Champions   BrainstormChampions.com
- Storytelling for the Revolution

        StorytellingForTheRevolution.com

MY BLOGS

- Storytelling   ideachampions.com/storytelling
- Innovation   ideachampions.com/weblogs
- Poetry   ideachampions.com/poetry
- Inner Self   ideachampions.com/heart
- Huffington Post   huffingtonpost.com/author/mitch-305

MY BOOKS

- *Storytelling for the Revolution*   On Amazon
- *Storytelling at Work*   On Amazon
- *Awake at the Wheel*   On Amazon
- *Full Moon at Sunrise*   On Amazon

CONTACT   mitch@ideachampions.com

Printed in the USA
CPSIA information can be obtained
at www.ICGtesting.com
LVHW090845140923
757945LV00001B/145

9 780996 912228